Xenophon

ANCIENTS IN ACTION

Xenophon

Fiona Hobden

BLOOMSBURY ACADEMIC
LONDON • NEW YORK • OXFORD • NEW DELHI • SYDNEY

BLOOMSBURY ACADEMIC
Bloomsbury Publishing Plc
50 Bedford Square, London, WC1B 3DP, UK
1385 Broadway, New York, NY 10018, USA

BLOOMSBURY, BLOOMSBURY ACADEMIC and the Diana logo
are trademarks of Bloomsbury Publishing Plc

First published in Great Britain 2020

Cover design: Terry Woodley
Cover image: Socrates discussing philosophy with his disciples,
Turkey 13th Century. (Photo by DeAgostini/Getty Images)

A catalogue record for this book is available from the British Library.

Library of Congress Cataloging-in-Publication Data
Names: Hobden, Fiona, author.
Title: Xenophon / Fiona Hobden.
Description: New York ; London : Bloomsbury Academic, 2021. | Series: Ancients in action | Includes
bibliographical references and index. | Summary: "This book offers a concise introduction to Xenophon, the
Athenian historian, political thinker, moral philosopher and literary innovator who was also a pupil of
Socrates, a military general on campaign in Persia, and an exile in residence in the Peloponnese during the
late fifth and fourth centuries BC. Alive during one of the most turbulent periods in Greek history, Xenophon
wrote extensively about the past and present. In doing so he not only invented several new genres, but also
developed pointed political analyses and probing moral critiques. It is the purpose of this book to explore
Xenophon's life, writing and ideas, and reception through thematic studies that draw upon the full range of
his work. Starting with his approach to the past and to Socrates, it demonstrates how the depiction of
events and people from previous times and places are inflected with contemporary concerns about political
instability and the challenges of leadership, as well as by a 'Socratic' perspective on politics and morality.
The following in-depth examination of Xenophon's theories concerning political organization and the bases
for a good life highlight the interconnectivity of his ideas about how to live together and how to live well.
Although Xenophon addresses conceptual issues, his writings provide a practical response to real-life
problems. Finally, an evaluation of his significance as an inspiration to later writers in their creative
interrogations of human affairs brings the investigations to a close. This book thus illuminates Xenophon's
importance within the vibrant intellectual culture of ancient Greece as an active participant in and evaluator
of his world, as well as his impact over time"– Provided by publisher.
Identifiers: LCCN 2020023399 (print) | LCCN 2020023400 (ebook) | ISBN 9781474298476 (paperback) |
ISBN 9781474298483 (hardback) | ISBN 9781474298490 (epub) | ISBN 9781474298506 (ebook)
Subjects: LCSH: Xenophon–Criticism and interpretation. | Historiography–Greece–History–To 1500. | Greece–
Historiography. | Greece–History–To 146 B.C.–Historiography. | Greek literature–History and criticism.
Classification: LCC PA4497 .H63 2021 (print) | LCC PA4497 (ebook) | DDC 938.007202 [B]—dc23
LC record available at https://lccn.loc.gov/2020023399
LC ebook record available at https://lccn.loc.gov/2020023400

ISBN: HB: 978-1-4742-9848-3
         PB: 978-1-4742-9847-6
         ePDF: 978-1-4742-9850-6
         eBook: 978-1-4742-9849-0

Series: Ancients in Action

Typeset by RefineCatch Ltd, Bungay, Suffolk

To find out more about our authors and books, visit www.bloomsbury.com
and sign up for our newsletters

To family and friends.

καὶ οὗτοι μὲν δὴ οὕτως ἀναμὶξ ἔσκωψάν τε καὶ ἐσπούδασαν.

'And so they joked and spoke in earnest, mixing it all up together.'

Xenophon, *Symposium* 4.29

Contents

Illustrations

Maps

Figures

Acknowledgements

It takes a long time to write a short book. So a colleague informed me, as I found myself still immersed in Xenophon's works three years after the commissioning of this book. Having finally reached the end, I am grateful for this restorative insight. Thanks are also due to Roger Rees for the invitation to contribute to Bloomsbury's 'Ancients in Action' series. The patience and commitment of the editorial team – Alice Wright, Lily Mac Mahon and Georgina Leighton – have been invaluable in bringing this project to completion.

One of Xenophon's key tenets is that the best way to learn anything is to seek out an expert. In coming to the University of Liverpool back in 2003, I inadvertently followed this advice. Not only was the university the home of Christopher Tuplin, who knows Xenophon well, but at Liverpool we are currently looking forward to welcoming old and new friends to our third international conference devoted to the author. The 'Further Reading' list at the end of this volume does little justice to the wealth and diversity of scholarship that is happening around the world now. My own readings of Xenophon's works have benefitted immeasurably from all this industry, as well as Christopher's intellectual generosity and warmth. Errors, of course, remain my own.

As this book has progressed, members of the clans Hobden and Montagnes have offered encouragement, enthusiasm and escape. My most heartfelt thanks are to David, who reminds me every day that there is more fun (are more puns) to be had than Xenophon.

Abbreviations

The following abbreviations are used in references to works by Xenophon (Xen.). Some texts are best known by their ancient Greek or Latin title, whilst some titles are more normally translated. This book follows common practice and, where necessary, gives English translations on first full introduction.

Ages.	*Agesilaus*
An.	*Anabasis*
Ap.	*Apology*
Hipp.	*Cavalry Commander*
Lac. Pol.	*Constitution of the Lacedaemonians*
Cyr.	*Cyropaedia*
Hell.	*Hellenica*
Hier.	*Hiero*
Mem.	*Memorabilia*
Oec.	*Oeconomicus*
Eq.	*On Horsemanship*
Cyn.	*On Hunting*
Por.	*Poroi*
Symp.	*Symposium*

Maps

Map 1 The Aegean in the fourth century BC.

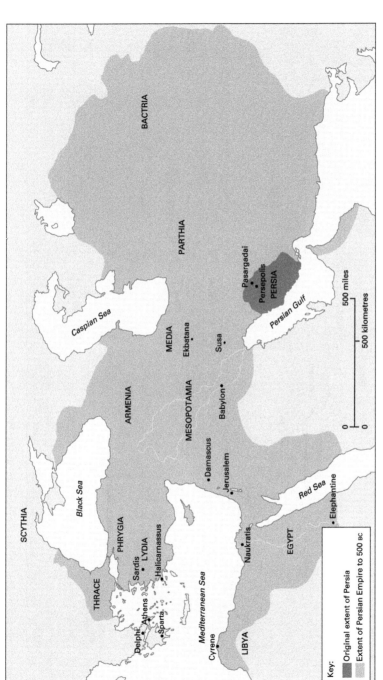

Map 2 The Persian Empire in the sixth century BC.

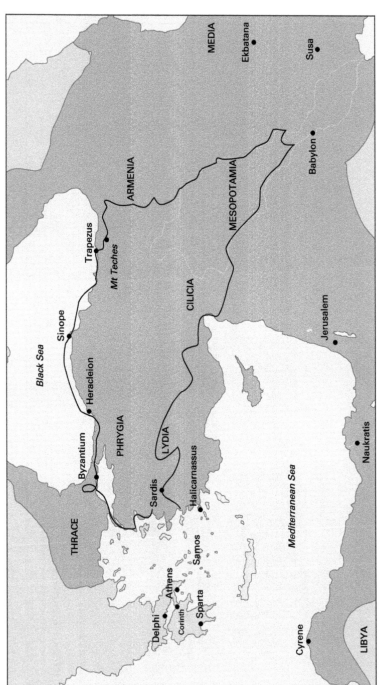

Map 3 Route followed by the Greek mercenaries in 401–399 BC.

Introduction

Words and Deeds

Xenophon the philosopher, a man unique amongst all other philosophers for adorning philosophy in both words and deeds.

Eunapius, *Lives of the Sophists* 453

Of the many individuals known from ancient Greece, Xenophon of Athens might appear the most accessible. With fourteen complete works surviving on topics as diverse as the education of the Persian king Cyrus, the virtues and value of Socrates, and the practicalities of cavalry command, the interests and opinions of the man seem clear. Likewise, from these same writings, it is possible to construct elements of his biography: as a pupil of Socrates, a military leader, and a man of letters and learning. Hence, we might think of him as Xenophon the Athenian, Xenophon the General, Xenophon the Historian, or Xenophon the Philosopher. Alternatively, to follow the favourable evaluation of ancient admirers like Eunapius, quoted above (see Chapter 5), he is a man of words and deeds. Each label captures an aspect of Xenophon's identity and outlook, making him readily comprehensible.

Yet, none of these assignations are as simple as they at first appear. Although he grew up in democratic Athens, Xenophon spent most of his adult life abroad, at first voluntarily and later in exile. By his own account, he was an accidental general, compelled by circumstances to take charge of a band of Greek mercenaries (known as the Ten Thousand) stranded in Persia after the coup they were hired to support failed. Indeed, the military life lasted only a decade, followed by a longer period settled in the Peloponnese. It is here that the majority of his works were probably written, and some may relate in content to his lifestyle and relationships at that time. But mostly his attention was projected backwards and outwards, his ideas and analysis honed through the construction of other people and past worlds. History and philosophy are intertwined in his imaginative explorations on topics of practical political and moral significance. Our easy categorization of Xenophon elides the complexity of his experience and outlook.

It is the purpose of this book to explore Xenophon through his writings and to get a measure of that complexity, for it is by understanding Xenophon in the round that his significance as an agent in and an observer of his contemporary world becomes clear. The remainder of this Introduction returns to Xenophon's biography, building outwards from the intimations in his written works towards the more elaborate accounts of later authors. It then sets out in fuller detail the character and range of his work, with attention to the mode and topics of investigation. This preliminary sketch paves the way for more detailed chapter studies on Xenophon's approach to the past, his presentation of Socrates, his political perspectives and his moral agenda. A final chapter then reflects on the impact of Xenophon beyond his death from antiquity to the present day. In many ways, Xenophon is a unique voice: a critical thinker whose distinctive life experiences facilitated a specific worldview that was elaborated through a series of innovative writing projects. And yet, he was very much of his time. By looking at the world through Xenophon's eyes, ancient Greece comes into focus.

Life stories

Anabasis, a narrative account by Xenophon of the march of that stranded mercenary army, offers some insights into the biography of its author. For a start, the book awards 'Xenophon the Athenian' a starring role in events following the defeat of Cyrus in his attempt to usurp the Persian throne in 401 BC. The young friend of a murdered Boeotian general, who is initially mocked for 'seeming like a philosopher' and being a fool (2.1.13), emerges as the principle leader of the army. Written in the third person, *Anabasis* depicts an able officer who navigates the vagaries of his troops and their ever-worsening circumstances to bring them back from the heart of Persia to the Mediterranean over the following year. However, it also provides a flashback of the same young man in Athens, 'neither a general nor captain nor common soldier', weighing up the original invitation from Proxenus to join him and seek Cyrus' friendship (3.1.4). The scene establishes Xenophon as an associate of Socrates, whose advice he seeks. Although that advice is only partially followed (see Chapter 2), its terms help define Xenophon's relationship with his home city. The Athenians, Socrates suggests, might not take kindly to someone joining up with the very Persian who supported the Spartans so enthusiastically in their war against Athens, a war that had ended in defeat for the Athenians only two years before (3.1.5). That the character Xenophon ignores Socrates' concerns, asking the oracle at Delphi not whether he should go but how, imbues the author's younger self with a disregard for and even antipathy to the city. It is striking in this respect that the *Anabasis* anticipates but does not depict Xenophon's return to Athens; convinced to stay with the mercenaries until the Spartan general Thibron arrives, the story ends at the point when the troops are integrated into his army. Whether Xenophon makes it back to the city where 'the vote against him concerning his exile had not yet been brought by the Athenians' remains unclear (7.7.57).

On the precise circumstances or cause of this exile, *Anabasis* remains coy. However, an episode during which monies from the sale of captives are divided up amongst the generals at Cerasus ends with reference to Xenophon's later deposit of a portion for safe-keeping with the priest at the temple of Artemis in Ephesus. This, it is reported, took place while Xenophon was travelling with the Spartan king Agesilaus from Asia to fight against the Boeotians (5.3.6). As is often noted, at this point in time Athens was allied with Boeotia in a coalition against Sparta. It is quite likely, therefore, that Xenophon took to the field against his fellow citizens at the battle of Coronea which took place not long after Agesilaus' return in 394 BC (described by Xenophon in *Hellenica* 4.3.15–20; the mercenaries who had followed Cyrus were amongst Agesilaus' forces: see 3.2.7). In addition, the return of this money and its use to fund an altar, temple and neighbourhood festival for Artemis on the river Selinus – the description of which briefly introduces Xenophon's sons – is prefaced by an explanation that during his exile Xenophon had been settled by the Spartans at Scillus, near Olympia (*An.* 5.3.7–10). Whether it was decreed before he befriended Agesilaus or after he fought with him, Xenophon's exile was spent in the territory and under the sponsorship of the Spartans, Athens' enemies.

The *Anabasis* is far from neutral in the presentation of its hero (see Chapter 1). Nonetheless, it provides a basic outline of Xenophon's life and prioritizes certain features: the relationship with Socrates, time spent in Persia with the would-be Persian king, disassociation and exile from Athens, military participation in and leadership of a Panhellenic venture, and close association with the Spartans. The first of these is also flagged during a series of dialogues that locate Xenophon in proximity to and direct conversation with the controversial Athenian philosopher. The most extensive of these,

Memorabilia, presents snapshots of Socrates in beneficial conversation with an array of young notables, as a way of countering the sorts of accusations that lead to his trial and execution in 399 BC. Amongst the future leaders and individuals familiar from the dialogue tradition, a youthful Xenophon is questioned on sexual desire and self-control (1.3.11). Elsewhere, the author situates himself on the edges, reporting what he once heard Socrates say on economics (in *Oeconomicus*) or at a drinking party (in *Symposium*), but otherwise playing no role in the conversation (see Chapter 2). While Xenophon's insinuation of himself into the Socratic circle is supported by his appearance, along with his wife, in a fragment from a lost dialogue by the philosopher Aeschines (quoted by Cicero, *On Invention* 1.31.51–2), it raises questions about his age. In the *Anabasis*, the character Xenophon raises his youth as a potential impediment to command (3.1.25). Yet, if Xenophon were around thirty in 401 BC, as this would imply – giving a date of birth *c.* 430 BC – he would have been very young at the time when Socrates attended Callias' drinking party, an event which the celebration of Autolycus' athletic victory in the Panathenaic Games places historically in 422 BC. Rather than solve the conundrum, it is sufficient to consider Xenophon a pupil of Socrates whose later reminiscences include a degree of inventiveness. A youthful association with Socrates is important in Xenophon's self-representation, situating him among a group of young men who were inspired by the philosopher and confounded by his execution, as the apologetic memorialization of their mentor in Socratic dialogues attests.

If Xenophon's year of birth must remain hazy, so too does the year of his death. Although the *Hellenica*'s chronological history of Greece ends in 362 BC, a direct allusion to contemporary circumstances allows him still to be writing between 357 and 353 BC, when Tisiphonus ruled Thessaly (6.4.37). The *Poroi*, furthermore, seems to reference the cessation of the Social War between Athens and its allies in 355 (5.12); its advice on Athens' management of resources fits right within this context (see Chapter 3). This puts Xenophon's latest works in the mid-to-late 350s. While it is noteworthy that even in his seventies Xenophon remained plugged into events unfolding around him, his advanced age means that he likely died not so long after that.

This synopsis of Xenophon's life can be supplemented by later tales. The third-century AD biographer Diogenes Laertius offers the most fulsome account in his *Lives of Eminent Philosophers*. Nonetheless, much of Diogenes' narrative elaborates upon elements drawn from Xenophon's own writing. For example, it opens with a vignette of the first encounter between Xenophon, son of Gryllus, and Socrates (2.6.48), in preface to the claim that Xenophon was the first writer of Socratic dialogues. The scene thus dramatizes the beginning of the relationship upon which Xenophon's conceit as an associate of Socrates and producer of dialogues depends. Next, Aristippus is cited as stating that Xenophon loved Clinias. This assertion is supported by a quotation extolling the beauty of Clinias, but in fact this is excerpted from a speech delivered by the character Critobulus in Xenophon's *Symposium* (Diogenes Laertius 2.6.49; Xen. *Symp.* 4.12; see Chapter 2). *Anabasis* is the source for information about Xenophon's decision to join Cyrus and serves as the basis for activities up until Scillus, whereupon Xenophon adopts a life of hunting, entertaining friends and writing histories (Diogenes Laertius 2.6.49–53). The portrait of a gentleman at leisure again reflects expectations arising from the very existence and specific contents of Xenophon's written corpus. So far, despite the dramatizations and conflations, Diogenes' biography of Xenophon looks very similar to our own.

There are some additional details, however. A wife called Philesia and two sons, Gryllus and Diodorus, are reportedly mentioned by Demetrius of Magnesia and by Dinarchus, the latter during a prosecution speech allegedly delivered on behalf of a disgruntled freeman (2.6.52). (Dinarchus was born *c.* 360, so whatever the contents of this lost speech, it is unlikely to have derived from an actual trial involving Xenophon.)

Diogenes also records the family's enforced departure from Scillus, when the area was seized by the Eleans (in the mid-360s BC), leading Xenophon to Lepreum and then Corinth, from where his two sons were sent to Athens to fight in defence of Sparta (2.6.53–4). The death of Gryllus on the battlefield at Mantinea in 362 BC is known to Diogenes through comments by the fourth-century historian Ephorus and allusions to contemporary speeches in his praise in Aristotle and Hermippus, including one by the Athenian pedagogue Isocrates (2.6.55). 'Such was his life', remarks Diogenes, before noting Xenophon's death at Corinth in a date that translates to 360/359 (2.6.55–6).

Diogenes' biography is worth treating at length because it illustrates the extent to which Xenophon's texts constrained the narrative of his life even in antiquity. And yet the basics were clearly expanded upon by later writers, so that a much richer story emerges. In the continuing discussion, Xenophon is rumoured to be the original publisher of Thucydides' history and alleged to be in open rivalry with Plato (2.6.57). Hellenistic epigrams, cited by Diogenes, extol his fame and record the warm welcome offered by Corinth to the Athenian exile (2.6.58). And accounts of that exile were embellished by a third-century historian Istrus, who added the proposer's name Eubulus to the decree of banishment, as well to a further decree supposedly rescinding it (2.6.59). All this additional information must be treated with healthy scepticism. Nonetheless, the diversity of narratives and sources that Diogenes draws upon indicates an abiding interest in Xenophon well beyond his own lifetime (see Chapter 5).

Life's work

The richness and variety of Xenophon's life is mirrored in the range and content of his writing. His corpus includes large-sale prose works centred on people and events from the distant and recent past, up to the present day (see Chapter 1). Of these, *Hellenica* (*Greek Affairs*) looks most like 'history'. Over seven lengthy books, and covering fifty years of Xenophon's own lifetime, it offers a relentless account of the fallings in and out of the Greek cities. Starting during the endgame of the Peloponnesian War and halting at the post-Mantinea impasse (411–362 BC), the narrative covers political and military events and shifts in alliances between the main players – Athens, Corinth, Sparta and Thebes – as well as interventions by the Persians and developments on the northern border with Thessaly (see Map 1). In the process it generates a moral critique of human motivation and action in the context of civil strife and shifting power relations. The bleakness of Xenophon's outlook here might be balanced against the idealistic approach to leadership found in *Cyropaedia* (*The Education of Cyrus*). For all it focuses on a historical personage, Cyrus the Great, founder of the Persian empire (*c.* 559–530 BC), the driving agenda and mode of delivery make it more akin to speculative fiction or biography: genres that *Cyropaedia* is arguably inventing. The work begins with the assertion that Cyrus obtained willing obedience in his subjects. Within the fantasy setting of the soon-to-be-conquered Assyrian empire, Xenophon elaborates within the framework of Cyrus' life to show how he accomplished this, from a childhood sojourn in Media with his grandfather, through military successes in Armenia, Hyrcania and Lydia, and on to the capture of Babylon (see Map 2). To some degree, *Anabasis* (*March up Country*) continues the investigation. Swaying between third-person travelogue and military memoir, following the Greek mercenaries as they fight pitched battle near Babylon, flee under Persian fire, retreat into the mountains of the Carduchi, push on through Armenia, and loan themselves out as bandits around the Black Sea and in Thrace (see Map 3), *Anabasis* explores the challenges of leadership. Here, the real-life difficulties experienced by Xenophon, as he attempted to marshal the troops through consistently dire circumstances, are channelled through the character of Xenophon.

Xenophon's exposition of historical scenarios and exemplary individuals is thus underpinned by a critical perspective. Each work may be different in form, subject matter and tone, but together they share an interest in personal morality, political action and leadership. The four Socratic works contribute to the same intellectual project. Zooming in on conversations between Socrates and the young men who gathered around him for instruction, these combine elements of dialogue and drama to portray philosophy in action (see Chapter 2). At one level these are all apologetic writings. Countering the charges of introducing new gods and corrupting the young that led to Socrates' prosecution, conviction and execution at Athens is the express purpose of *Memorabilia*. Cumulatively, the forty-nine reported conversations create a portrait of Socrates as a man of exemplary virtue who fostered moral excellence and devotion to useful service in his followers too. At the same time, *Memorabilia* builds its own perspectives on a wide range of moral and political questions through the interlocutions between the philosopher and his pupils. *Oeconomicus* (*On Estate Management*) and *Symposium* (*The Drinking Party*) extend the portrait and the examination of philosophical ideas by showing Socrates instructing and receiving instruction on household management and contributing to the wit and repartee at a drinking party hosted by the wealthy Athenian Callias, respectively. *Apology* (*Defence*), by contrast, gives an account of Socrates' conversations before and after his trial, and of his performance in the law court. These last two works share titles with dialogues by Plato. However, in terms of methods and ideas, Xenophon's Socrates is distinct from his Platonic counterpart. Yet, the question arises how far the ideas imputed to Socrates are original to the philosopher. There are striking continuities between the arguments afforded to Socrates and premises explored elsewhere in Xenophon's writings: for example, on political participation and living a good life (see Chapters 3 and 4). In Xenophon's mental modelling, Socrates is always a ghost in the machine.

This is perhaps clearest in Xenophon's encomiastic portrait of Agesilaus II (*c.*445–359 BC). Whilst the extended praise awarded to the Spartan king automatically aligns him with the mythological characters or war dead who were its usual recipients, his core virtues – self-control, moderation, endurance, love of toil – are those of Xenophon's Socrates. However, this is not their limit, and, importantly, Agesilaus demonstrates his virtue through his treatment of others as king (Chapter 4). Whatever the similarity, attributing 'Socratic' virtues to Agesilaus is only a starting point for Xenophon in building a model of excellence in leadership. This is true too for *Hiero*. Here, the poet Simonides takes on the role of Socrates in interrogating Hiero I of Syracuse (ruling 478–466 BC) on his experiences as a tyrant, before suggesting how he might govern more successfully. However, the proposition that tyranny functions best as a reciprocal relationship between a ruler and his subjects is distinctive to Xenophon. *The Constitution of the Lacedaemonians* is another theoretical treatise on political organization. Xenophon appears to be following Socrates' lead – or at least the lead given to the young Pericles by the philosopher in *Memorabilia* (4.4.15) – by endorsing customs established by Lycurgus that instil obedience to the law. However, the vision of Sparta encompasses all elements of society, recording Lycurgus' directives on education, women, government, law and the military. Xenophon's favoured polity is a surveillance society (see Chapter 3).

Across his writings, Xenophon is concerned with human affairs, especially the relationship between the individual and the community. Although written in a more didactic fashion, Xenophon's technical treatises share this concern. *On Hunting*, for example, promises to transform its young readers into men of virtue who will benefit their hometown and win honours if they put its lessons into practice (see Chapter 4). *Cavalry Commander* is pitched to a reader charged with maintaining their city's mounted troops. Writing with a view towards Athens, Xenophon offers guidance on satisfying the Council and nurturing loyalty alongside matters of training and deployment. Here, Xenophon adds his wisdom to a pool of writing on similar topics. *On Horsemanship* is intended for the private reader (12.14), yet it is concerned with mounting and fighting, and its instruction is arguably foundational to success in hunting and cavalry command. All this applied knowledge has a practical goal, which, although unstated, supports Xenophon's wider proposition that a good man serves his community. It is a position the author consciously adopts when he presents his recommendations for raising funds. *Poroi* (*Ways and Means*, or *Revenues*) is directed to Athens at a time of financial difficulty (in 355 BC). The hinterland, resident foreigners, the port and markets, the silver mines, and slaves could all yield extra resource, if Xenophon's proposals for exploitation are adopted. Late in life, possibly returned from exile if the recommendations for what 'we' should do are taken at face value, Xenophon sets himself up as a wise advisor to his home city.

This is Xenophon in action: thinking through and finding solutions to practical problems relating to politics and morality. Before progressing further, it must be noted that there is another way to interpret Xenophon: as a clever manipulator whose writings possess hidden meanings for a knowing reader to recognize. This approach originated in the mid-twentieth century with the German-American political philosopher Leo Strauss (1899–1973). Adopting his method of 'reading between the lines', others have followed in arguing that Xenophon fundamentally problematizes Lycurgan Sparta, or consciously undermines Cyrus' supposedly model rule, for example. In short, this very modern Xenophon is a deconstructionist who pulls apart his surface hypotheses to create damning exposés, rather than a constructive thinker, working through problems towards solutions. The implications and significance of Strauss's work constitute an academic field of study by themselves, and this is not the place to rehearse the ins and outs of arguments. Instead, three points are worth making.

First, Xenophon was one of several thinkers from intellectual traditions reaching from antiquity to modernity whose works Strauss considered esoteric: i.e. who used strategies such as contradiction, ambiguity and paradox to signal hidden meanings in order to evade open declaration of unpalatable views. At the same time, Strauss elevated 'reading between the lines' into his primary critical mode. Thus, by making Xenophon ironic, Strauss sublimated him to a broader world view. Second, for deliberately hidden meanings to have effect, they must be recognisable to a reader who is able to spot and decipher telltale dissonances that others cannot, as a result of special knowledge. Aside from the fact that nobody thought to look for these before the twentieth century (see Chapter 5), there must be serious concerns regarding the modern reader's ability to identify and interpret them, given our lack of training. When the meaning of the text is to be extrapolated, there is no way of checking the legitimacy of our extrapolations. Third, scanning for apparent disjunctions, ironic readers tend to focus exclusively upon the text, losing sight of the interconnections between Xenophon's different works, as well as the socio-political world in which he was writing. A holistic reading of the corpus, of the sort exemplified by Vivienne Gray in *Xenophon's Mirror of Princes* (2010), demonstrates a strong degree of continuity in thinking by Xenophon about his contemporary world. For example, in *Memorabilia* the character Socrates presents a nutshell version of the argument pursued Xenophon's *Constitution of the Lacedaemonians* (see Chapter 3). An ironic reading of the latter would require a reassessment of Socrates' argument at this point, even if that is not internally cued. In short, consistency would break down entirely if what Gray calls 'darker' readings of sporadic texts were allowed stand.

By reading Xenophon's works in turn and together, this book eschews the negative interpretation fostered by twentieth-century political science in preference for the sort of contextualized close readings generally preferred by Classicists. Taking its cue from the ancient identification of Xenophon as a 'man of words and deeds', its Xenophon is a constructive writer who is preoccupied above all with the best ways for individuals and communities to behave. Certainly, Xenophon's conclusions are not always straightforward: for example, when his enthusiasm for Sparta wavers in the face of recent exploits (see Chapter 3). Sometimes Xenophon can be playful: for example, when Socrates, having been lured to Callias' drinking party on the promise that his host will display his wisdom, ends up teaching his host how to educate his boyfriend for a life of political service; or when Lycon, one of Socrates' prosecutors, praises his future opponent on leaving Callias' drinking party (*Symp.* 1.6, 8.6–43; 9.1) (see Chapter 2). (There is irony here, but it is obvious and humorous, rather than hidden and consequential: what Gray describes as 'light' instead of 'dark'.) In other places, pessimism breaks through. The Greek cities fail to break the cycle of war; and through personal experience Xenophon knows how difficult it was to keep the Greek mercenaries together (Chapter 1). Moreover, Xenophon openly recognizes the contestability of his own presentation, in his encomium of Agesilaus at least (Chapter 4). Rather than being problematic and destabilizing, such equivocations are part of a textured whole. Over and over, Xenophon comes back to two fundamental questions that look towards a better future. How might we live together and how should we live well? These will be anchoring points in the coming investigation into Xenophon's thought world.

1

Writing History

The ancient Greeks possessed a rich historical imagination. Through the public performance of poetry and plays to the sculptures that adorned temples and decorative scenes on domestic drinking vessels, exceptional deeds were retold, restaged and displayed. The expeditions against Troy and its heroes' protracted returns, the adventures of Heracles and of Theseus, the internal conflicts that over generations brought down the ruling houses of Mycenae and Thebes: such stories projected discrete and interconnected pasts for Greek communities, conveying contemporary values and providing a route to self-identity. By the fifth century, recent events were supersized into this mythical register. So, Aeschylus presented the Athenian victory at Salamis in 480 BC in tragic form (*Persians*, produced 472 BC), and in verse Simonides (*Elegy* 11) compared the Spartan-led victory at Plataea the following year to accomplishments at Troy. At the same time, historiography, the writing up of authored inquiries into the recent past, elevated its subject matter: thus Herodotus addressed 'the great and marvellous deeds done by Greeks and non-Greeks' (*Histories* 1.1) whose fame he sought to preserve, and Thucydides aimed to create a 'possession for all time' by recording a conflict that was 'great and noteworthy above all other wars' (*History* 1.22, 1.1). These two authors – each known today as a 'father of history' – also interrogated imperialism through their separate depictions of the Persian Wars and Peloponnesian Wars. Imagining the past was an opportunity for celebration, reflection and critique.

When Xenophon wrote about the past, he entered this tradition. By providing accounts, respectively, of Greek relations from the

Peloponnesian War to the destruction of Sparta (411–362 BC), the education of Cyrus and his rise to the Persian throne (*c.* 540 BC) and the journey of a Greek army stranded in Persia (401–399 BC), *Hellenica*, *Cyropaedia* and *Anabasis* each commemorated the deeds of exceptional individuals in conflict situations. Furthermore, they also advanced a critical position. As this chapter will show, by capitalizing upon new historiographical techniques, Xenophon simultaneously imposed a coherent narrative upon the past and articulated his concerns as an inhabitant of the present. Writing history offered a means to analyse contemporary Greek politics, model good leadership and explore associated difficulties, with insights afforded through active reflection and first-hand experience. Human action and motivation sit at the heart of this analysis. In their depiction, Xenophon fluctuates between pessimism and idealism.

On Greek affairs

Befitting its title, Xenophon's *Hellenica* presents a concentrated study of 'Greek affairs'. At its core stand Athens and Sparta, whose antagonism and changing fortunes provide the context for myriad conflicts between Greek cities. The primary terrain of activity is the Aegean, from its islands to the coastal and inland settlements of the Greek mainland (see Map 1). It also extends up and over through Thessaly, Macedonia and Thrace and across the Hellespont into Asia, from where Persian satraps intervene, as well as westwards to Sicily, whence Dionysius sends reinforcements, including Celtic cavalry. Events thus unfold in an interconnected Mediterranean world. This combination of singular focus and breadth of scope is also a hallmark of the *Hellenica's* temporal purview. Progressing forward, *Hellenica* zooms in on one location to describe military confrontation or political decision-making at one point in time before moving on to another, following a sequence of episodes or shifting to a new stream. Characterized by the frequent refrain 'after that' (*meta de tauta*), the narrative of Greek history thus moves horizontally (across space) and vertically (down time), cumulatively tracing human activity around the Aegean over a fifty-year period. In the process, events are depicted, motivations are asserted, consequences are detailed, and judgements are implicitly invited or explicitly made. *Hellenica*'s account of recent Greek history is also a critique of human affairs.

To understand this critique, it is necessary to appreciate Xenophon's technique. Like any historian, Xenophon is the architect of the past that he seeks to represent: he selects what to write and how to write about it. For *Hellenica*, the frame is set by a pervasive focus on conflict which prioritizes the actions of individuals and communities in times of war. This is exemplified already in the first paragraph of *Hellenica*, which picks up where Thucydides left off (in 411 BC):

> After that, and not many days later, Thymochares came from Athens, bringing a handful of ships. Immediately the Lacedaemonians and Athenians entered battle once more, and the Lacedaemonians won, led by Agesandridas.
>
> *Hellenica* 1.1.1

The Athenian and Spartan crews fight it out, but it is the intervention and skill of their respective leaders that provoke battle and facilitate the outcome. A 'Great Man' view of the past is mitigated somewhat by the diverse cast of named individuals drawn from multiple cities, the majority of whom make only brief appearances. Nonetheless, in *Hellenica* men in charge make events happen. This is not simple chauvinism, however. A person-centred approach helps Xenophon navigate a complex and fluid military-political scenario. The effect can be seen as the sequence of events unfolds. Moving on into winter, the main actors are: Doreius, bringing ships from Rhodes and then beaching them under Athenian attack at Rhoeteum; Mindarus at

Ilium sailing to the rescue; Alcibiades arriving in the Hellespont with ships to support the Athenians; Pharnabazus leading his troops to aid the Spartan fleet, as it flees towards Abydus; and, finally, Thrasyllus departing to report to Athens, whilst the majority of Athenian ships sets out from Sestus to requisition money (1.1.2–8). The location and movement of these persons within the north-eastern Aegean defines the field of military action. At the same time, the focus on individuals keeps the story moving, with new arrivals facilitating successes and reversals in fortune for the undifferentiated troops serving under them.

The reactions of individuals to developing circumstances also create drama: for example, when the sight of the sea battle causes Mindarus to launch his triremes (1.1.4), or Pharnabazus rushes on his horse into the sea and fights, cheered on by his own cavalrymen and foot soldiers (1.1.6). Although brief, these are heroic moments, during which single men step to the fore and into danger. However, a character in the *Hellenica* is just as likely to respond to circumstances with a speech. For example, when the Spartan general Callicratidas finds himself undermined by the allies of Lysander, whom he has been sent to replace (in 406 BC), he makes an address to the Spartan fleet that describes his assumption of command as an act of obedience. With the spectre of the state's authority raised, dissent is quashed (1.6.5–6). Or next, when he fails to extract money from the Persian king, Callicratidas extorts funds from a panicked Milesian assembly by exhorting them to show leadership amongst the allies and join Sparta in punishing their enemies. With this injection of cash, Callicratidas can now attack and remove Methymna from Athenian control (1.6.8–14). In both instances, the way forward is disputed. Callicratidas' arguments override the opposition and effect a solution. In *Hellenica*, the persuasive speaker is as much the agent of history as the general who charges onto the beach. And yet, in both cases the self-interest of the listeners, who (as stated or implied) dare not challenge the authority of the Spartan state or are alarmed at the demand to go to war, is as much a factor in what happens next. Thus, in addition to showing how events unfolded, by staging deliberation and reporting outcomes, *Hellenica* offers insights into why they happened.

The organization of Xenophon's history around the (inter)actions of cities, led by individuals who stand apart from and act on behalf of the community, makes *Hellenica* a fundamentally political work. War dominates not on its own merit (as in Thucydides' *History*), but as the acting out of shared and conflicting interests between networks of allies or factions within a city. This is exemplified by events following the arrival of Timocrates of Rhodes in Greece in 395 BC with fifty talents of silver, provided by the Persian satrap Tithraustes. Timocrates' advent ultimately results in conflict between Corinth, Thebes, Argos and Athens on the one side and Sparta on the other. However, there are various motivations at play. First (as reported), Tithraustes intends to divert the Spartan king Agesilaus from his conquests in Asia by stirring up trouble at home. Second (as implied), the named individuals who take the money and discredit Sparta in their hometowns are motivated by greed. Third (as stated), it is hatred that pushes the first three cities into alliance (3.5.1–2). Fourth, when the Thebans then act provocatively, this becomes a pretext (as described) for the Spartans to punish Thebes for earlier acts of insolence (3.5.4–5). Fifth (as demonstrated), the Athenians are persuaded into alliance by promises of renewed supremacy and out of gratitude for the Thebans' earlier rejection of a Spartan plan to attack Piraeus (3.5.8). Competing ambitions over wealth and power, be they long-standing or freshly inspired, result in the ongoing breakdown of relations within and between cities.

Hellenica charts the violence that follows. An initial assault by Sparta on Haliartus, designed to provoke the city into breaking its allegiance to Thebes, results instead in the Spartans' rout by the

Thebans and their withdrawal from Boeotia, following a further battle
with the Athenians (3.5.16–25). Once Agesilaus arrives, more victory
trophies are set up for the Spartans than their enemies: at Corinth
(4.2.23), in Thessaly (4.3.9), and against massed forces at Coronea
(4.2.23, 4.3.9, 4.3.21). At the same time, however, Spartan ships are
defeated in a naval battle with the Athenians and Persians at Cnidus
(4.3.10–12). In short, none of the victories is conclusive. An authorial
perspective might be found in the concluding summary for a battle
that arises when Sparta and the Sicyonians attempt to seize Corinth at
the request of some exiles (in 392 BC). 'On that day, in a short period
of time many fell, so that men accustomed to seeing mounds of grain
and wood and stones, instead saw mounds of corpses' (4.4.9–12). By
imagining the perspective of the farmer transplanted onto the
battlefield, the narrator conveys the scale of the slaughter. As in
the *Iliad*, where the worlds of agriculture and war are frequently
juxtaposed to problematize heroic action on the battlefield, this
comparison evokes *pathos*, an emotional response to human suffering.
The epic allusion carries forward the problematics of war. This element
is deepened by the battle's inconclusive result. Practical outcomes
include a tactical retreat by Sparta, following some localized
destruction, and the establishment of garrisons in the region, with
Theban troops installed at Corinth and Spartan ones at Sicyon
(4.4.13–14). However, with mercenaries fighting on both sides, and
further assaults and invasions, the war continues with victories and
losses all round.

The sensitivity Xenophon shows to the human impacts of war is
even stronger in his depiction of events at Corinth, prior to the battle.
The slaughter of peace-seeking Corinthians by those with a vested
interest in continuing the war against Sparta, not least the men in
Tithraustes' pay, is clearly coded as an atrocity. Judgement builds
initially in the description of the targets as 'the most and best of the
Corinthians' and those who fled as 'the best men'; and, subsequently,

in the opposite presentation of the perpetrators and their plan as 'most impious of all'. Such moralizing is reinforced by a sensationalist account of how the victims were slain, detailing where they were killed and what they were doing. Also highlighted are the facts that the undertaking took place on a festival day – indeed, judges in theatrical competitions were amongst the dead – and that the killers, showing no regard for the law, murdered those who sought sanctuary at the statues and altars. The reported despair of onlookers at the unfolding sacrilege reinforces the narratorial judgement and evokes pity, as does the numbering of old men amongst the dead. Finally, the motive awarded to Pasimelus and Alcimenes, the young exiles who later appeal to Sparta for help, is that they observed those with power ruling tyrannically and recognized in this the eradication of their city (4.4.1–7). Authorial comment, the careful selection of language and staging of events, the evocation of pity and the imbedding of mutually reinforcing perspectives through witness response mark the actions of the Argive-backed regime at Corinth as deplorable.

The effect is strengthened, moreover, by resonances with earlier events at Athens, when members of the Spartan-appointed oligarchy turn to mass murder (in 404/3 BC). In this episode, the actions are critiqued through competing speeches from two prominent members of the junta. Critias argues that eliminating opponents is key to the oligarchs' survival, whereas Theramenes presses for restraint on the basis that killing good men weakens the state by robbing it of their services and fostering hostility (2.3.15–49). In this account, it is Theramenes who receives the applause of the Council, and whose perspicuity of mind in death, following conviction at law by his rival, merits direct praise (2.3.50–6). Moreover, it is on Theramenes' execution that the oligarchy of the Thirty is said to transform itself into a 'tyranny', expelling citizens and seizing their property: exactly the sort of behaviour that Theramenes had described as the 'worst injustice'. Significantly, this is the same terminology the narrator uses to describe the proscriptions by Critias and the Thirty (2.3.22, 2.3.43, 2.3.17), who are themselves 'most sacrilegious' (2.3.53). At Corinth and Athens, local men establish select governments that use violence to eliminate the innocent and pursue their own agenda, backed by external regimes who intervene to serve their own interests. The murderous excesses of the impious Corinthians are drawn retrospectively into alignment with the injustices of the Athenian oligarchs.

The different roles played by Sparta in both episodes highlights the role of expediency in determining foreign policy. Support for the oligarchs at Athens consolidates their victory over the city; supporting the Corinthian exiles is a means of continuing the fight against the enemy coalition. However, while the actions of the Greeks might be governed by pragmatism, for Xenophon, history is underpinned by a moral imperative. Hence, in the midst of describing how, following the eventual subjection of Thebes, Corinth and Argos, leaving Athens bereft of allies, 'their [the Spartans'] rule seemed without a doubt to have been established securely and well' (5.3.27), Sparta's impiety and its ultimate defeat are flagged. Indeed, the subsequent narrative of reversal is presented as evidence that 'the gods do not overlook the sacrilegious nor those who commit unholy acts'. The Spartans' offence is to have broken their oath to uphold each city's autonomy by seizing the acropolis at Thebes (and, indeed, handing it over to men who would be tyrants). Thus, when the Thebans under the command of Epaminondas defeat the Spartans at Mantinea at the end of *Hellenica* (7.5.18–25), they effectively exact punishment as 'victims of injustice' (5.4.1).

The Greek affairs that Xenophon narrates are thus characterized by change. Competing interests and shifting alignments within and between cities, exacerbated by the intervention of external powers, result in continuous conflict. The cessation of violence is only ever temporary. This is emphasized by the forward-moving chronology and the frame of progression established by that regular *meta de tauta* refrain, 'after that'. Notably, what follows is invariably more violence. Indeed, the final *meta de tauta* occurs in the very last sentence, when the narrator declares, 'Let matters up to this point be written be me; what happens next (*ta meta de tauta*) may perhaps be of concern to another' (7.5.27). Just as Xenophon took up Thucydides' account, the historian passes on the baton. However, the statement follows directly upon an assessment of Greek affairs that emphasizes the confounding of expectations, disorder and confusion. Instead of the stronger force establishing itself as ruler over the defeated following the battle of Mantinea, both sides claimed victory, whilst nonetheless failing to advance their own position. Here, 'the god' is directly credited. As a result, what occurs is 'the opposite of what all men believed would be': and so 'confusion and disorder were greater still after than before the war in Greece' (7.5.26–7). Across fifty years, nobody emerges triumphant. On the best reading, despite the constant shifts on the ground, nothing has changed in the Greek world; and on the worst, matters have deteriorated. It is significant, perhaps, that in the *Poroi*, written around the same time as *Hellenica* (see Introduction), and after further conflict between the Greeks within Athens' allied network in the Social War, Xenophon actively endorses peace (see Chapter 3). For now, at the end of *Hellenica*, the author seems to break off in despair.

Modelling Persian kingship

Like *Hellenica*, Xenophon's *Cyropaedia* combines direct report, dramatic sequences, set-piece speeches, interpretative statements and evaluative judgements to create a forward-moving narrative informed by a person-centred approach. By contrast to the wide scope and underpinning pessimism of Xenophon's Greek history, however,

Cyropaedia is a singular and idealizing account of Cyrus' transformation from precocious princeling to savvy king. In narrative terms, the terrain through which Cyrus marches is a testing ground for the young Persian prince; but the conjured world is also a testing ground for Xenophon's theories on leadership. This interest is established by *Cyropaedia*'s opening frame, which styles the forthcoming story as the continuation of a prior conversation (linking it to a culture of philosophical discourse more commonly exemplified by Xenophon's Socratic works: see Chapter 2). Essentially, by inculcating willing obedience across a vast polyglot terrain populated by cities and tribes, Cyrus confounds the agreed principle that ruling men is impossible. What follows is then the result of an earlier investigation into the nature and education that enabled Cyrus to exert his rule (1.1.1–6). This includes not only consideration of Cyrus' character and his experiences as a youth (book 1), but demonstration of how formative traits and understandings underpinned interactions with everyone Cyrus encountered as he progressively expanded his power to defeat the incumbent Assyrian king and implement his own rule (books 2–8). The work ends, moreover, with an assessment of how subsequent kings failed to follow Cyrus' approach to their detriment. *Cyropaedia*, the title of which means 'education of Cyrus', comprises simultaneously a personal history (or biography) for Cyrus, a record of the formation of the Persian empire and an interrogation of how to govern well.

This integrated approach may be exemplified by tracing forward two bases for Cyrus' success identified in the preface: namely his manipulation of fear and favours (1.1.5). The former is evidenced across Cyrus' military career. His first military venture, aimed at recouping tribute owed to his uncle Cyaxares, the king of Media, is successful because Cyrus anticipates that fear will motivate the wrongdoing Armenian king to flee. He thus directs troops to intercept the household personnel and treasures sent ahead to safety by the king and thereby compels his submission (3.1.1–4). This understanding of how people respond to fear also informs Cyrus' campaigning strategy. Soon out marching with Cyaxares, Cyrus argues that to withhold their troops from view will inspire greater fear amongst the enemy than to line up immediately against them, because the enemy will remain uncertain about the Medians' capabilities (3.3.30–2). Conversely, Cyrus later recommends a direct march upon Babylon, even though their force is small. The purpose is threefold: to avoid giving the impression of fear, to capitalize upon the fear resulting amongst the Assyrian forces from their recent defeat, and to minimize fear amongst Cyrus' crew (5.2.31–7; see also 6.2.13, 7.5.20). Cyrus' mastery of the psychology of fear, as revealed by these practical measures, also underpins his approach to military training. As he explains to Chrysantas, fear can only be overcome by a learned ethos that 'the greatest happiness belongs to good men of good report' (3.3.53.). Without rigorous training and living examples of this, men will always value their own lives above the promise of praise in death (3.3.51–5). As if in confirmation, when Cyrus' well-drilled men find themselves enclosed by forces under the Lydian king Croesus, led on by Cyrus, they advance despite their great fear. The enemy, by contrast, flees (7.1.23–6). Whether it is to be inspired or overcome, fear is key to Cyrus' success: a hypothesis that is revealed over the course of the *Cyriopaedia* through its subject's assertions and proven through his accomplishments.

The principle of inspiring obedience through favours, the second basis for Cyrus' success, is likewise exemplified across the *Cyropaedia*. The sojourn into Armenia on Cyaxares' behalf is again formative. During the trial of the renegade Armenian king, the son Tigranes convinces Cyrus to spare his father from death by arguing that in future fear and gratitude will make him a good friend (3.1.24–31). Once accepted, Tigranes' lesson plays out well for Cyrus, when the Armenian king pledges troops and money. Moreover, it also advantages the Armenians, because Cyrus uses those resources to broker peace with the Chaldaeans, thereby fulfilling a promise to benefit his new friends. Now, the Armenian king has gratitude for the 'good things' Cyrus has accomplished, and which shame dictates he must return (3.2.16, 3.1.34). What begins as an act of justice morphs into a reciprocal relationship. Indeed, it continues when Tigranes joins Cyrus on campaign and receives a share of booty to redistribute and a robe for his wife. The former follows an attack on the enemy camp, while the latter is offered during a victory feast at Babylon, where Cyrus' four most committed friends are rewarded (4.2.18, 4.2.42; 6.1.21). The two-way relationship between Cyrus and the Armenian royal family persists to their mutual benefit.

The lesson Cyrus learns in Armenia and applies during his campaigns is, however, also the realization of ideas exchanged in a pre-campaign conversation between Cyrus and his father Cambyses, the Persian king. The first, offered by Cambyses, is that an army guarantees an individual's willingness to gratify due to their fear of what might otherwise follow. The second, proposed by Cyrus in response, is that the army is an instrument by which to act on behalf of friends and receive their help in return (1.6.10–11). As well as setting the basis for events in Armenia, this understanding inflects Cyrus' every encounter with a potential-enemy-turned-friend. In fact, final victory over the Assyrian king is made possible because of Cyrus' commitment (in terms of fourth-century ethics, a very Greek commitment) to helping friends and harming enemies. When Cyrus arrives with a victorious army in tow, Gobryas and Gadatas are brought on side through promises of not only power and wealth (see 4.6.8, 5.2.7–8. 5.3.2–5, 5.3.9–14), but revenge (4.6.2–8, 5.2.28). Their local knowledge enables Cyrus to enter Babylon with his troops, where the two men and their followers slay the king (7.5.24). Gobryas and Gadatas avenge the murder of their sons, and Cyrus takes the throne. In this model of friendship, founded again upon gratitude, the different parties agree to serve each other's interests in order to fulfil their own. This a lesson with its roots further back in Cyrus' childhood: when the young prince recognized that his agemates would find another to press their case if he would not persuade his grandfather Astyages to take them hunting in the wild (1.4.11–12). By taking the story forward from there to Cyrus' conversation with Cambyses and to his future encounters on campaign, *Cyropaedia* illustrates how the king-to-be established willing obedience by forming relationships informed by fear and based upon aligned self-interest.

Applied equally to the army, who are motivated to strive for excellence by rewards in training and in the field (2.1.22–4, 30; 2.3.2–16), and to his appointed subordinates, who the king keeps in his debt by always offering greater services (8.2.12), these principles are foundational to Cyrus' success. However, Cyrus also benefits from personal qualities instilled in childhood through formal education. As abstractly described, the stepped system of training by age groups inculcates martial ability and moral probity in the sons of the Persian nobility. Incorporating practical lessons in justice, a boy's education up to the age of seventeen focuses on moderation, obedience and self-control, each of which is learned through observation of their elders (1.2.8). Ten years of public service spent in the city and out hunting then hones the young men's expertise in weaponry and their physical endurance, so that by the age of twenty-five they are ready for military service (1.2.3–13). This is an education in virtue (*aretê*), or so the Lydian king Croesus describes it, contemplating the inevitability and justness of Cyrus' usurpation and his own defeat (7.2.24). Cyrus' victory is enough to recommend the model. And indeed, it is one the new king seeks to implement. Moderation, self-control and hard work will be key to maintaining authority, he declares to friends and allies, whilst simultaneously inviting them to embrace an invigorating life of toil and the pursuit of manly excellence (7.5.75–6, 80, 82). By his plan, the nobles and their sons will live at court as they would in

Persia, with the former checking themselves against the model offered by Cyrus, and the latter learning by their example (7.5.85–6). It is an effective strategy. Or so the author confirms when he states that examples set by Cyrus in moderation and self-control so inspired discipline, deference, decency and emotional restraint that any court observer would conclude everyone was living 'a good life' (8.1.30–3).

Cyropaedia thus moves from the explication of fundamental childhood lessons towards their demonstrated fulfilment. Again, this final implementation follows an intermediate stage of exemplification. For example, Cyrus' moderation in food and drink is particularly emphasized through a series of banqueting vignettes. The first takes place on the young Cyrus' arrival at Astyages' royal court in Media. Here, citing the simplicity of Persian fare, Cyrus distributes his share of the many dishes on offer to his grandfather's attendants, thereby displaying control of bodily appetites and anticipating his later commitment to rewarding good service (1.3.4–7). Cyrus then wittily recalls the chaos of a previous drinking party: with participants 'poisoned' by the wine, the conversation entirely broke down into solipsistic shouting, risible singing, boasting, dancing and free speech, all of which disrupts the power hierarchy (1.3.10). The boy's seemingly naïve interpretation reinforces the contrast between the unrestrained feasting and drinking of the Medes and his Persian self-control.

Unsurprisingly, such exuberance is absent from all Cyrus' parties, which instead involve enjoyable and stimulating conversation (as asserted at 2.2.1 and 2.3.1 and demonstrated inbetween). Furthermore, on occasion, Cyrus encourages his men to postpone eating and drinking following victory until further work has been done; and they eat abstemiously then return to service while others dine (4.2.39–46, 4.5.4–6). Significantly, following this latter occurrence, the narrative segues to Cyaxares, who emerges from drunken celebrations only to learn that his soldiers have departed with Cyrus: 'So the Persians spent their time; but the Medes feasted sumptuously and drank and listen to the pipes and took their fill of all good cheer' (4.5.7–8). Cyaxares experiences a loss of men and of face because he sends his nephew out to hunt down the fleeing enemy, whilst he prefers to party (4.5.9–10; 4.1.13–22). Overindulgence undermines military capability. Then again, for Gobryas, the simplicity of the setting and food and the measure of the Persians in their consumption and conversation reveals a simple fact: that 'we' are inferior because we seek to enrich ourselves, whilst 'you put effort into making yourselves better men' (5.2.14–20). A simple life inculcates virtue. Cyrus' career trajectory is evidence of its benefit.

When Cyrus establishes a Persian-style education at court, the *Cyropaedia* comes full circle to its point of departure and appears to anticipate the future replication of his utopian regime. However, this is not the end of the story. Rather, a deathbed speech during which Cyrus reiterates the importance of helping friends and punishing enemies (8.7.7, 13, 28) is capped by reports that his sons fall out, the cities and tribes secede and 'everything turned to the worse' (8.8.2). *Cyropaedia* ends with a litany of failure. Alongside the corruption of the honours system, the pursuit of wealth through injustice, and the diminution of the army (8.8.5–7), the Persian nobility now prefer eating and drinking over toil. Future generations make use of the very couches and coverlets that Gobryas noted for their absence and they indulge in the many delicacies that the young Cyrus found so problematic (8.8.8–13, 15–19). Cyrus' great accomplishments last only so long as the king.

This is the inevitable conclusion to an investigation premised upon the exceptionality of its subject. Befitting its originating impulse and its title, the *Cyropaedia* shows how lessons learned by Cyrus in his youth were applied with consistency during his military career and resulted in his installation as king. Cyrus' success within his own lifetime endorses the founding principles of his rule. In the final evaluation, though, what matters is the character of the ruler: 'for whatever sort of man their leader is, such will those under him become' (8.8.5). From the very first Cyrus is superlative 'by nature': 'most beautiful in form, most generous, most learned and most loving of honour' (1.2.1–2). And further virtues are recognized by the people he encounters. These include wisdom, strength, kindness, beauty and greatness, according to the Armenians whose king is spared lethal justice (3.1.41); plus, exceeding piety, moderation and compassion, according to the captive Panthea, who recruits her husband to Cyrus' cause (6.1.47). To the newly allied Hyrcanians, Cyrus' strength of spirit is a source of wonder (4.2.14); whilst to his friend Artabazus, Cyrus is the most beautiful and best of men (4.1.24). The virtue of the Persian king is consummate. Without his example for imitation Cyrus' system collapses. Thus, the enervation of the Persians after Cyrus is not so much a slight on that system as testimony to its susceptibility to human nature. On the question of whether it is possible for one man to rule another, the pessimism of the discussion group that *Cyropaedia* strives to overcome may still be the appropriate response.

Stepping into history

Differences between the *Hellenica* and *Cyropaedia* illustrate the malleability of historiography in the fourth century BC, as well as their author's skill and flexibility. Although built using the same set of tools – narrativization, dramatization, speechifying and authorial direction – each work conjures up a distinctive world within which relevant issues play out. Thus, where *Hellenica* generates a critical perspective on the conflict-torn Aegean of recent Greek history, *Cyropaedia* shapes the emergent Persian king Cyrus into an ideal leader. Xenophon's *Anabasis* likewise shifts focus and expands the agenda. The topic is the 'march up country' (*anabasis*) of the Greek mercenaries on campaign with the young pretender Cyrus, and their struggle to return home once their paymaster is killed in battle against his brother Artaxerxes, the king, near Babylon. Despite lacking the moralizing interventions of the *Hellenica* and authorial framing of *Cyropaedia*, *Anabasis* generates a perspective on leadership in a 'real life' setting by centring its quasi-epic story of return on the words and deeds of another emergent leader: Xenophon the Athenian. While there is certainly a self-promotional element in the depiction of the author's younger self in action, the difficulties the new general experiences trying to keep the Greek army together and bring it back safely exemplify a realist understanding that chimes with *Hellenica* and *Cyropaedia*.

On the development of this leadership theme, it is important to note that for the first two books of *Anabasis*, the character Xenophon is virtually absent. Instead, book one begins with a Persian royal family drama. One the one hand, the wrongful arrest of Cyrus by Artaxerxes on suspicion of sedition after their father's death (1.1.1–6) establishes a historical background for the Greeks' service in the rebel army. On the other, it explains the motivations of Cyrus, who in many ways this wider section is about. Thus follows an account of the measures Cyrus takes to muster forces (1.1.6–1.2.3); the route he charts through Lydia and Cilicia towards Babylon, leading, amongst other things, to a romantic entanglement with the wife of a local ruler (1.2.12, 1.2.26–7); the obstacles he faces, including the satrap Tissaphernes' continuing opposition (1.2.4), a mutiny by the Greeks (1.3.1–20) and a relative's betrayal (1.6.1–11); and his preparations for and eventual death in combat (1.7.1–1.8.27). This is crowned with an extended eulogy of Cyrus, which begins with his description as the 'most kingly' and 'most worthy to rule' since the elder Cyrus (i.e. the subject of *Cyropaedia*) and continues by delineating the outstanding qualities of this would-be Persian king. Of particular note, considering that comparison, are Cyrus' military capability and trustworthiness and his propensity to benefit friends, punish wrongdoers and reward distinction (1.9.1–31). Through this elevation, *Anabasis* signals the qualities of the best kind of ruler, albeit one who is let down by a heroic but ill-advised leap into the fray of battle.

This diversion from the main action anticipates an authorial assessment of the Greek generals lured to their deaths by Tissaphernes (2.5.30). Here, however, the positives are consistently balanced against negatives. Clearchus the Spartan displays a warlike spirit, a love of war, and a harsh disposition, but his propensity towards violence undermines his troops' affection and loyalty (2.6.1–15). For Proxenus the Boeotian, a softer man, an unwillingness to punish wrongdoers means that only the best men follow him, even though he understands the importance of contracting friendships as a result of his sophistic education (2.6.16–20). In the balance, neither quite gets it right. Then again, Menon the Thessalian is the worst kind of leader. Being driven to rule and to acquire honour by greed, Menon formed friendships that enabled him to commit crimes with impunity, and he mocked and deceived men who exhibited higher principles (2.6.21–7). At this point in the story, the Greeks have been negotiating their departure from Persian territory (book 2). The generals' murder leaves the remaining Greeks in a state of perplexity (3.1.2), and with a power vacuum to fill. Taken together, these various character summaries set behaviours for any future leader to aspire to or avoid, and against which they might be measured.

The individual who fills the gap is the character Xenophon. Although his earlier appearances were brief, hindsight reveals their significance: connecting him to Cyrus and the mission's divine sponsor, when he seeks instruction from Cyrus before battle and delivers the watchword 'Zeus, Saviour and Victor' (1.8.15); or showing his devotion to the Greek cause on attending a meeting of the generals in the immediate aftermath of Cyrus' death (2.1.12); or placing him in the company of his soon-to-be murdered friend, Proxenus, with whom he detects plots by Ariaeus, a former Persian ally (2.4.15,

2.5.41). In terms of character building, all of this is a productive preliminary to the moment when Xenophon steps forward into action and into history. This is a moment of high drama. A lengthy sentence depicts in detail the Greeks' languor and despair: stranded in hostile territory without allies or horses and longing for home, no-one can bring themselves to light a fire, let alone eat or sleep (3.1.1–3). Except for Xenophon. Invigorated by a dream of lightning and fire that he interprets as a message from Zeus, Xenophon addresses first Proxenus' captains, then all the remaining generals and captains, and finally the entire army (3.1.11–37). This man, who joined as 'neither a general nor captain nor soldier', but at the invitation of Proxenus and to seek the benefits of friendship with Cyrus (3.1.4; see Introduction), motivates everyone to action. Stepping forward thus initiates a transformation in Xenophon's status. Having previously faced mockery from Phalinus, the Greek representative of the Persian king, as a foolish young man who speaks like a philosopher (2.1.12), now, following his rousing speeches, Xenophon is universally acclaimed as the new commander of Proxenus' contingent (3.1.24–6). Furthermore, he is praised for both his words and deeds by the Spartan general Chirisophus, who is joined by the soldiers in endorsing Xenophon's plans (3.1.45–6; 3.2.33). Thereafter, Xenophon-the-general sets the agenda for the army and dominates the narrative.

With this development, the *Anabasis* shifts more definitively towards a portrait of leadership in action. Not all the qualities exemplified by Cyrus or the murdered Greek generals are easily possessed. For example, Xenophon's first independent military action is a failure. Pursuing Persian horsemen by foot is a futile gesture that raises the ire of the other generals. However, a contrite Xenophon then orchestrates a more successful plan: to form a unit of Rhodian slingers and a cavalry comprised of horses pulled from the baggage chain (3.3.9–20). The value of the latter is shown in the repulsion of Mithridates' next attack (3.4.3–5), while Tissaphernes' soldiers will shortly fall back when the Rhodian slingers return fire, putting an effective end, together with a team of bowmen, to the enemy's skirmishing (3.4.14–18). Xenophon is learning. Indeed, he is soon permitted to enact his own plan to seize a high summit in order to dislodge the enemy from their current position above the Greeks but lower down the hill. Addressing the men with a stirring speech from his horse, Xenophon later joins them on the ground in a race to the hilltop (3.4.38–49). With his military credentials thus established, and as the Greeks advance into the territory of the Carduchi, Xenophon increasingly works in tandem with Chirisophus from their customary positions in the rearguard and the van, whether claiming high ground to force passage or fording a difficult river (4.3.24–6, 4.3.13–34). Their strategic competence and practical manoeuvres keep the Greeks moving onwards through hostile territory.

Above all in these endeavours, Xenophon dedicates himself to the soldiers' survival, whilst also leading by example. When the winter cold brings lethargy, sickness, frostbite and snow-blindness, he is the first up to cut wood for a fire, he personally collects and distributes food to the afflicted, and he protects those who are unwilling to carry on, before forcing them to persevere (4.4.12–13, 4.5.7, 4.5.15–22). Later, called to trial, Xenophon defends himself against accusations of wrongdoing in exactly these terms. He did strike soldiers during this difficult stage of the march, but not due to arrogance. Rather, he punished those who abandoned companions and sought to keep others moving and out of enemy hands. Thus, Xenophon saved the men who now complain of brutality (5.8.1–26, esp. 17–18). Likewise, towards the end of the march, when unpaid soldiers accuse Xenophon of growing wealthy under the patronage of the Thracian warlord Seuthes at their expense, Xenophon refutes the allegation. Had he not abandoned plans to leave the army in favour of making himself useful, when he learned that the troops were in danger (7.6.11; see 7.2.5–9, where the Spartan commander at Byzantium, Aristarchus, plans to enslave them)? In addition to escaping this fate, the soldiers have also benefitted from regular provisions and the glory of victory which the resulting alliance with Seuthes has brought (7.6.31–2). Seuthes' irritated description of Xenophon as being too 'friendly to soldiers' is a further line of defence (7.6.5, 39). The appeal ends with a recap of all that Xenophon has suffered 'with you', and the benefits conferred, right up to the soldiers now being in a position to accept the offer brought by those Spartans to join their general Thibron in a new Persian campaign (7.6.3–7). In both instances, Xenophon's successful self-defence confirms what has already been illustrated: namely his commitment to the common good.

That Xenophon needs to defend himself from such accusations reveals underlying difficulties. Not everyone interprets his actions in the right way; and opponents collude against him. Events following the Greeks' arrival at the Black Sea are especially revealing, anticipating as they do the first trial. Here, a pernicious rumour spreads regarding Xenophon's private desire to establish a colony and so 'win territory and power for Greece' (5.6.15). Under pressure, Xenophon publicly renounces the plan. However, there is more to this dissent than the troop's wish to return home. Silanus, the seer employed by Xenophon to read the omens, is concerned about getting his savings safely back to Greece. The merchants and representatives of Sinope and Heracleia to whom Silanus talks are motivated by fear to offer bribes to several of the Greek generals. Financial considerations thus influence the negative presentation of Xenophon's ambitions to the assembled soldiers by those generals, one of whom, Thorax the Boeotian, is also a long-standing rival of Xenophon (5.6.16–5.7.11). Various interests, personal and political, external and internal to the army, coalesce into a concerted attack on Xenophon's authority. Finding himself out of synch with the wishes of the majority, Xenophon can only counter this by agreeing to the soldiers' demands (5.6.31).

Furthermore, as the army struggles onwards, division in the ranks accelerates. For, despite the rousing emotion of the moment when the Greeks catch a glimpse from Mount Teches of 'The sea! The sea!' (4.7.24), the return to the Black Sea does not put an end to the soldiers' journey or their hardship. Instead, the failure of local communities and the Spartans who control the region to furnish ships and resources to take their fellow Greeks home traps the army into forming friendships with barbarian tribes (of which Seuthes in Thrace is only the last example). Raiding the lands of their enemies for provisions that are increasingly difficult to come by, the soldiers continue to suffer and die. Under this pressure, the army even splits for a time along city lines (6.2.4–16). When the Spartans, in cahoots with the Phrygian satrap Pharnabazus, later block their progress, the generals reach an impasse. Should they join Seuthes (as proposed by Phrynichus and Cleanor, in anticipation of reward from the Thracian warlord), advance to the Chersonese (where the Spartans might sanction Neon's full command), or cross into Asia (bringing Timasion home to the Troas, where he had earlier promised everyone would find wealth)? Responding to the inertia, soldiers drift away (7.2.1–4; 5.6.23). In these circumstances, Xenophon struggles to keep the army together and to maintain his position, and even considers leaving on several occasions (6.2.15, 7.1.4, 7.1.38, 7.7.57). And yet, motivated again by a desire to protect his men, Xenophon ultimately stays the distance and achieves an end goal: not actually reuniting them with their friends and family, but depositing the soldiers with the Spartan general Thibron (7.7.57, 7.8.24), thus 'uniting' them in the Greek army and returning them to the fight against the Persians: the only workable solution.

In *Anabasis*, leadership is a challenge. Over the course of the march, Xenophon comes to display some of the positive qualities attributed to Cyrus and the dead generals: especially military skill, and a concern to benefit his men. However, just as competing interests keep the Greek cities at war in *Hellenica*, manoeuvring by individuals within the Greek army create difficulties for the young general. Whereas in the imagined Persian past depicted in *Cyropaedia*, similar principles of leadership enabled Cyrus the Great to obtain willing obedience as sole ruler, present-day realities hinder this achievement by Xenophon. Indeed, invited by the soldiers to become their general-in-chief, Xenophon turns them down. On the one hand, the decision is made easy by unfavourable omens; but in refusing the offer, Xenophon points both to the likelihood of hostility from the Spartans to his appointment (detrimental to his own safety and the progress of the march) and to the anger and internal strife that will likely follow it (6.1.17–31). The truth of the latter is proven when the Spartan Chirisophus is chosen instead (6.1.32–3). His appointment is immediately undermined by the Arcadians and Achaeans, who negotiate independently with the Heracleots and then form their own break-away unit. Chirisophus' generalship lasts only seven days (6.2.4–12). Thus, amongst the Greeks in the here-and-now, single rule is an impossibility. Xenophon cannot fulfil Cyrus the Great's trajectory. Instead, his story ends with a final raid against a wealthy Persian called Asidates. Awarded first pick of the booty by his comrades, Xenophon now has the resources to keep fulfilling his previous imperative: 'to do good for others' (7.8.8–18). Exile may be looming (7.7.57), but this for now is a happy ending.

Conclusion

Whether writing about Greek affairs, the rise to power of the Persian king or the travails of the Greek army on route through Persia, Xenophon creates a narrative about the past that engages critically with the present. His person-centred accounts respond to questions about human behaviour and motivation that reflect the complications and messiness of the real world. In *Anabasis*, the character Xenophon struggles against the self-interested machinations of rival generals who destabilize his leadership and foster disunity within the army to their own advantage, reflecting in microcosm the wider tendencies amongst the Greeks in their internal and foreign relations exemplified in *Hellenica*. Both these works address recent history, and Xenophon's lived history, and must be informed by his experiences as an inhabitant of and agent in the world. Only *Cyropaedia*, which resurrects the temporally and geographically remote Persian past, allows for the attainment of stability and prosperity, although with the passing of time the Persian monarchy will weaken, as evidenced further in the brotherly rivalry and military weakness that underpin the *Anabasis'* depiction of the Persian empire today. What is needed, Xenophon suggests, are good leaders. What that leader might be, *Cyropaedia* works through. But even its author seems unconvinced by his own model. It takes an exceptional individual to compel willing obedience. Xenophon's younger self struggles to meet the challenge and wins only in a limited sense, handing the surviving Greeks (about half those who originally joined Cyrus) over to Thibron. With the majority opposed to him founding a colony, Xenophon will never test his potential for sole rule, although he will carry on doing good to his friends. Furthermore, in a situation marked by moral failure and perpetual violence, there seems little scope for altruistic leadership within or between Greek cities. The completion of *Hellenica* towards the end of Xenophon's life may suggest a movement towards pessimism, fostered by a backwards review with the endpoint of Spartan defeat in view. Given uncertainty over the relative composition dates, however, it is impossible say more about specific developments in Xenophon's thought. Rather, each of Xenophon's historical writings should be regarded as an intervention: an illustration of how things were that reflects how things are, whilst implicitly or explicitly encouraging thinking about how they might otherwise be.

2

Remembering Socrates

In 399 BC, Socrates son of Sophroniscus was executed by the Athenian state, following prosecution at law. As laid out by Xenophon, the charges were not believing in the city's gods, introducing new gods and corrupting the young (*Mem.* 1.1.1). Pursued in the aftermath of their city's devastating defeat by Sparta and its divisive civil war, the trial may have been a cathartic moment for the Athenians. The guilty verdict effectively eliminated a man with disruptive methods and ideas, whose known associates had been prominent in two short-lived but bloody oligarchic revolutions in 411(part-orchestrated by Alcibiades) and 404/3 BC (led by Critias). To Socrates' disciples, by contrast, it was a terrible injustice. Unable to affect the outcome, they began instead to write. In the decades that followed, numerous accounts of the conversations of Socrates circulated, effectively constituting a post-trial defence. Thanks to the manner of his death and the response of his followers, the ideas of a man who left behind no written texts were committed to posterity. Plato was the most prolific author of these so-called Socratic dialogues; but amongst the many individuals who together produced hundreds of scenes, the only other known follower of Socrates whose works have survived intact is Xenophon.

Xenophon's Socratic works were thus contributions to a developing project with a radical agenda: to provide a counter-version to the prevailing narrative involving Socrates. For Xenophon, this meant portraying Socrates as someone who brought benefit to those with whom he associated, making him a positive influence and thereby a force for good within the city. Across the *Memorabilia, Oeconomicus, Symposium* and *Apology*, Socrates is depicted conversing with notable youngsters on topics of moral and political significance. By consequence, each work also develops philosophical perspectives. Selected and fashioned by Xenophon, the 'recorded' conversations thus contribute to the author's own wider project as it developed through and extended beyond his Socratic works. To fully map Xenophon's imaginative engagement with his departed mentor therefore requires attention both to how Xenophon constructed his 'Socratic dialogues' and mounted a defence, and to the philosopher's more ephemeral and idiomatic presences. For Xenophon, remembering Socrates was a permanent state of mind and an ongoing process.

Dialogue or drama?

In producing his Socratic dialogues, Xenophon may have had other models to guide him (disregarding Diogenes Laertius' claim he invented the genre: see Introduction). Even in their absence, though, his experimentation and innovation are clear. *Symposium*, *Oeconomicus*, *Memorabilia* and *Apology* are united by the presentation of Socrates in conversation. How they do this, however, varies. The first three are all first-hand accounts: or at least they purport to present the author's recollection of prior occasions when he witnessed Socrates in action ('I was present': *Symp.* 1.1, *Mem.* 4.3.2; 'I heard': *Oec.* 1.1, *Mem.* 1.4.2, 2.5.1; 'I remember', *Mem.* 1.3.1; 'I know' 2.9.1, 2.10.1, 3.3.1, 4.4.5, 4.5.2). But even here there is diversity. *Symposium* describes a drinking party at which Socrates' voice is one amongst many and his offerings form only part of the evening's entertainment. *Oeconomicus* provides a more intimate portrait of a one-to-one conversation between Socrates and Critobulus, which incorporates and concludes with Socrates' report of an earlier exchange with Ischomachus. Structured more like a Platonic dialogue in this respect, *Oeconomicus* also comprises an extended version of the shorter discussions between Socrates and his young acolytes that pack out the *Memorabilia*. However, *Memorabilia* also begins and ends with an authored exculpation of Socrates from the charges laid against him, and it includes repeated pointers towards the right interpretation of Socrates' ideas and intentions. *Apology*, by contrast again, expands upon a closing strategy in *Memorabilia* by drawing upon Hermogenes' account of Socrates' words before, during and after his trail (*Mem.* 4.8.4–11). Thus, each recollection of Socrates is distinct in its approach, but these works are also intertwined. Only in the final two are apologetic ambitions explicit.

As this variety indicates, Xenophon's Socratic dialogues are more than simple transcripts of things Socrates once said. They are authored and self-authorizing accounts that zoom in on the philosopher and his companions meeting and conversing within distinct scenarios. *Symposium* is particularly notable for developing a dramatic setting. It begins with the wealthy Athenian Callias inviting Socrates and his associates to accompany him and his friends to a party at his home, where they are joined by a laughter-maker and a troupe of hired entertainers. Assembled, the guests switch between enjoying the entertainment and making their own conversation. *Apology* too offers context. In addition to setting up an exchange between Hermogenes and Socrates in advance of the trial, it describes Socrates' courtroom performance, including the jurors' jeering response and Socrates' cross-examination of the prosecutor Meletus, plus the departure of the condemned man and his emotional farewell to followers after being convicted. While scene-setting in *Oeconomicus* is restricted to an assertion of authorial presence, which by inference situates the two speakers in a bigger group, the *Memorabilia* is occasionally more descriptive, bringing Socrates and his companions to a saddler's shop to converse with Euthymedes (4.2.1, 8), or to the home of the courtesan Theodote (3.11.1–2), or to a dining club (3.14.1), for example. Xenophon's Socratic works thus comprise a series of vignettes. In their most elaborated form these approach drama, with physical settings and the participants' words and actions evoked in the mind's eye. Indeed, reading practices may have enhanced this dimension by transforming the written text into an oral performance and audial experience. With the words of Socrates and his interlocutors spoken aloud to listeners, each reading would become a re-enactment of the conversations 'remembered' by Xenophon.

Philosophy in action

In the opening section of *Memorabilia*, Xenophon defends Socrates against charges of impiety by emphasizing that his interest lay in human affairs, and not the more controversial areas of natural philosophy or cosmology. Thus, he asked 'what is' piety and impiety, beauty and ugliness, the just and the unjust, self-control and madness, bravery and cowardice, the city and the statesman, a governor and government. The aim of interrogating these and other such topics was to generate understanding of human behaviour, and in the process to make the inquisitor *kalos kagathos*, literally 'beautiful and good' (1.1.11–16). Led by Socrates, conversation is a tool for moral improvement. To achieve this aim, Xenophon later asserts, Socrates' preferred method was to solicit agreement on a question from his interlocutor and thereby travel forth towards the truth (4.6.14–15). Hence, on the topic of impiety, Socrates begins by asking Euthydemus, 'Tell me, of what sort do you consider piety to be?' To Euthydemus' answer that it is the 'most beautiful thing', Socrates then poses another question about the sort of man who is pious, which leads Euthydemus to describe him as one who 'honours the gods'. This causes Socrates to inquire whether he honours them willingly; Euthydemus explains there are laws. There then follows a series of propositions from Socrates that demand and receive his interlocutor's assent ('I believe so', 'Absolutely', 'How could it not?', and so on) to the building notion that a pious man is one who worships as he should according to the laws that he knows. And from here Socrates proceeds with a series of directed questions that establish the definition of a just man (who also knows the laws), and of wisdom (which involves acquiring knowledge), and of the good (which is useful), of beauty (also useful), and of courage (also beautiful, and the product of knowledge) (4.6.2–11). In this way, understanding of human affairs is developed incisively and cumulatively. In addition, whenever Socrates deemed his interlocutor's argument deficient, he would lead them back again to the fundamentals (4.6.13). It was by this sort of drilling, Xenophon asserts, that Socrates honed his companions' dialectical skills (4.6.1).

The approach is familiar to the *Oeconomicus*, which launches with an interrogation of the sort of knowledge that is called 'estate' or 'household management' (*oikonomia*), executed through questions that invite explication and assent. Socrates again takes the lead, and again the responses by Critobulus are crucial in shaping the conversation, both in their substance and in the stimulus they provide to Socrates' further questioning. At points Critobulus even prods Socrates more critically: for example, inviting him to defend his preference for poverty (2.1–19), or challenging his claims about the farming practices of the Persian king (4.5). And Critobulus repeatedly seeks to direct Socrates back to the solicited topic of growing one's estate, when Socrates divulges the necessity of freeing oneself from bodily desires (2.1), or offers guidance on gaining knowledge from experts in crafts that are not estate management (4.1), or leaves practical matters behind to talk about the gods and the benefits of farming (6.1, 6.9). In other words, the conversation is collaborative.

That is not to say Socrates does not maintain the upper hand. For example, Critobulus finds himself unable to argue against Socrates' observations regarding the pitfalls of wealth (2.9), and although at first dubious, he acknowledges the Persian king's care for the land

(4.5; 4.12, 14, 17). Furthermore, there is something comical about Critobulus' tussle to regain control over Socrates' apparent digressions, the significance of which he does not quite grasp. Ultimately, Socrates dominates the conversation, not just through the length and intellectual force of his contributions, which reveal limitations in Critobulus' understanding and focus, but also by delivering a monologue that makes up the full second half of the work. Even here, however, the mode is interrogative: for this monologue presents a conversation between Socrates and Ischomachus. Having previously elicited guidance on estate management from a man deemed to be *kalos kagathos*, Socrates now passes on his advice, preserving the original question-and-answer format. Through this sustained representation of Socrates in action, *Oeconomicus* extends the method summarized in *Memorabilia* and witnessed in small-scale interlocutions, realizing its richness and complexity.

The *Symposium* offers a further showcase for the interactive dimension to Socratic discourse. As befits a drinking party where the 'playful' and 'serious' deeds of men who are *kaloi kagathoi* are on display (*Symp.* 1.1), spirited conversation flows between the host and his guests, with short exchanges following the drinking pattern of 'small cups and often', a strategy recommended by Socrates for the greatest merriment (2.26). Yet, just as he assumes control of the drinking, Socrates also directs events, insisting even on the benefits of conversation over the pleasures offered by the hired dancers (3.2). Despite having been reluctant to attend Callias' party, he effectively becomes its leader, or symposiarch. Under Socrates' guidance, physical performances stimulate light-hearted conversations that facilitate pronouncements on the pursuit of *kalokagathia* (the quality distinctive to the *kalos kagathos*), the teachability of women, and the benefits of exercise (§2). Speakers expounding their greatest knowledge are prodded and teased by Socrates, who, with the help of Antisthenes, light-heartedly points out inconsistencies in their logic

(§§3–4). Socrates also enters into a beauty competition with Critobulus, during which he attempts to convince the judges of the superiority of his satyr-like facial features – the protruding eyes, flaring nostrils, snubbed nose and large mouth – based on their utility: a reappraisal of beauty with which Critobulus is compelled to agree (§5). Socrates even acts as a guardian of the sympotic conversation. An invitation to a truculent Hermogenes to describe *paroinia* paves the way for Socrates to chide him for fulfilling his own definition of the word by 'annoying others over wine'; and the Syracusan impresario and the laughter-maker Philip are both chastised for deficiencies in their supposedly humorous conversation (§6). Socrates next encourages a singsong and offers a critique of the acrobatic entertainment (§7). Stimulated by the current gathering where the god Eros presides, Socrates then embarks upon a lengthy monologue that examines the nature of love and promotes it as a route to virtue (§8), directing his lesson towards the host Callias (8.11, 28, 37). This is Socrates' last spoken contribution; his final act is to leave the party when it breaks up, following a raunchy pantomime that enthuses some guests – but not Socrates – to rush home to their wives (§9). In sum, although everyone freely participates, Socrates controls the conversation. With the shape and contents of that conversation informed by the sympotic occasion, productive interrogation and deconstruction are combined with assertive statements and a lengthy monologue. Following the tendency of the symposiasts to mix up joking with earnest speaking (4.29), *Symposium* delivers serious critique via Socratic play.

Thus, within the variety of interactions presented across Xenophon's dialogues, a consistent portrait emerges of Socrates in action. For readers familiar with the Platonic dialogues, it is noteworthy that Xenophon's Socrates makes only limited use of *elenchus*, a style of a cross-examination that involves the refutation of another's position. It does seem to have been part of Socrates' imagined toolkit, with Critias and Alcibiades reportedly resenting having their errors exposed in this fashion (*Mem.* 1.2.47; cf. 1.4.1). And thwarted on an earlier occasion by Socrates' *elenchus*, Aristippus seeks to turn the tables by carefully working out likely answers for questions about 'the beautiful' and 'the good' in order to have ready responses that can prove Socrates wrong next time around (3.8.1). However, while Plato's Socrates frequently uses *elenchus* to reduce his interlocutor to a state of *aporia*, whereby there is no way forward with an argument (in the early dialogues at least), in the one instance where he employs it, Xenophon's Socrates does so constructively. For Euthydemus, mentioned above, exposure to his own ignorance under interrogation (recognized at 4.2.23, 36, and 39) was the first step towards further association during which Socrates 'most simply and clearly related that which he believed it was necessary for him to know and to be the best practices' (4.2.40). Here, *elenchus* constitutes an invitation to philosophy, rather than a discrete mode of inquisition.

This assertion stands in counterpoint to the accusation by the sophist Hippias that Socrates questions and refutes and laughs at everyone else without ever making clear his own view (4.4.9). Not only is Hippias shown to be wrong in the interrogation which immediately follows, when the allegation that 'what is just' equates to 'what is lawful' is clearly espoused and proven (4.4.12–25). More generally, many conversations in *Memorabilia* end with clear statements of principle that might even guide future action. So, for example, Socrates' discussion with his son Lamprocles on the definition of the ungrateful man and the role of parents ends with positive encouragement to Lamprocles to cease being disgruntled with his mother, lest he be judged ungrateful by men and gods (2.2.13–14). The newly elected general Pericles is exhorted by Socrates towards actions that will 'bring honour to you and good to the state', and to support their shared wish that that city become stronger (3.5.27–8; see Chapter 3). Then again a peaky-looking Epigenes is told to do some exercise, for being in prime condition is not only useful on the battlefield, but also enables a person to best help their friends and the city, to win honour and to thereby enjoy a better life (3.12.4). If the young men implement Socrates' practical instructions, then well-being will follow for the individual, within the family and in the community at large.

As in these three instances, Socrates' lessons often arise in response to immediate situations. Repeatedly, the observation of an individual's problems with friends and family or of their ambition for or elevation to a civic role or of their immediate state of mind or body inspires Socrates to initiate conversation and offer solutions. Such a positivistic presentation again distances Xenophon's Socrates from his Platonic incarnation, in that Plato's protagonist sometimes pretends a lack of knowledge or will say something other than he means. Certainly, under the influence of Plato's Socrates, which has led such 'irony' to be regarded as a 'Socratic' trait, a similar dissimulation has sometimes been read into Xenophon's Socratic works, especially the *Oeconomicus*, following the lead of Leo Strauss (see Introduction). However, in *Memorabilia*, it is both demonstrated and stated (at 4.7.1) that Socrates reveals his opinions clearly. This straightforward approach fits Xenophon's presentation of Socrates as useful to those who sought him out precisely 'so that they might become *kaloi kagathoi* and be able to do good service to their house and household and friends and the city and citizens' (1.2.48). Socrates' lessons on human affairs are not decontextualized analyses of abstract phenomena. Nor are they replete with esoteric meanings. Rather, conducted in a straightforward way, they serve a practical purpose.

Defence

Within the above sketch of Socrates' method, it is possible to discern the basis of Xenophon's defence. Misunderstood and misrepresented,

Socrates in fact spent his life engaged in useful pursuits. Hence, it is exactly in terms of his utility to others that his teachings are first introduced in *Memorabilia* (1.3.1). Far from corrupting the young, Socrates leads his friends to become *kaloi kagathoi* and to possess *kalokagathia* (*Mem.* 1.2.7, 1.6.14). This he achieves by offering instruction on behaviour that is unbefitting to those aspiring to such status and virtue (for example, sexual incontinence: 1.2.29, 1.3.11), as well as instilling the necessity of temperance (2.1.1) and actively making his companions better (1.2.61, 1.4.1), increasing their piety and prudence (4.3.18; on the latter cf. 1.5.1), and causing them to become more just (4.4.25). But more generally, offering his own model of moderation through abstemious living (1.2.1–2; 1.6.1–10), Socrates prioritizes this virtue as a necessary antecedent to cleverness, effectiveness and resourcefulness. Without it, such abilities might otherwise be used in service to injustice and wrongdoing (4.3.1; cf. 1.2.17, addressing Alcibiades and Critias). The starting point is always attention to the gods (cf. 1.4.2–18). Far from being a radical innovator or an iconoclast, Xenophon's Socrates is a moral and pious man who trains his followers accordingly (1.4.19).

Memorabilia thus offers a holistic defence of Socrates by refuting the charges laid against him whilst demonstrating his worth. As dramatizations of Socrates' fruitful engagements, the same might generally be argued for *Oeconomicus* and *Symposium*. Of particular note, the final section of *Symposium* opens with praise: 'By Hera, Socrates, you seem to me to be man who is *kalos kagathos*' (9.1). Spoken by Lycon, these words have special resonance. In the future, beyond the imagined moment of sympotic frivolity, Lycon will play an active role in Socrates' trial. By making him assert Socrates' excellence, in terms that echo and thereby substantiate the *Symposium*'s opening claim that the words and deeds of *kaloi kagathoi* are worthy of recall (1.1), Xenophon playfully transforms the real-life prosecutor into an admirer of Socrates. At this point, Socrates has just finished advising Callias on how best to prepare his beloved Autolycus for a life of virtue and public service. This includes, for example, by practising virtue and providing instruction (8.27, 39), the very sorts of activities the *Memorabilia* accredits to Socrates in person. With this knowing inversion, Xenophon awards Socrates the consent of a father who will later accuse him of corrupting the young.

In the *Apology*, by contrast, Socrates speaks for himself, albeit with his voice mediated through Xenophon's report of Hermogenes' account. Unlike the wide-ranging *Memorabilia*, and befitting its short length, the purpose is narrowly set: to explain how Socrates' defence has been misconstrued as boastful speaking (§1). Convinced that the blamelessness of his life is the best defence, Socrates prefers to weary the jury with a demonstration of his good fortune and self-worth and thereby choose to die at a timely moment, rather than to live into a reduced old age (§§2–9). So, in court, attending carefully to the charges, he offers his public worship of the gods as testimony to his belief, interprets the claim regarding new gods as the result of a misunderstanding over his guiding spirit, and explains his excellence – as recognized by the god Apollo who declares no other man to be more free, just or moderate (§14) – as the basis for taking over the education of young men from their family (§10–21). The jurors react with an outcry of disbelief and envy. As Socrates later remarks to his companions, his conviction, in the end, resulted from false witnesses, who are guilty of impiety and injustice, rather than Socrates, against whom none of the charges were proven. Thus, he meets death assured both of its injustice and that time will show 'I have never made anyone worse, and I benefitted those who conversed with me, without reimbursement, teaching as I was able about the good' (§26). Thus, Socrates' self-exculpation matches the terms of Xenophon's wider defence.

The *Apology* explicitly sets itself up in competition with other accounts of Socrates' defence, which must include Plato's *Apology*, and which might have extended to circulating versions of the prosecution speech, such as the *Accusation of Socrates* attributed to Polycrates by Isocrates (possibly of a slightly later date). Where Xenophon notes that much more was said than he reported (§22), the difference between the speeches given by Socrates in the two surviving *Apologies* – regarding, for instance, the functioning of Socrates' guiding spirit as a dissuader from rather than persuader to action, and the contents of the Delphic oracle, which by Plato's account recognizes Socrates' wisdom (Plato, *Apology* 31d, 40a, 40d; 21a) – emphasizes a point signalled already by the differences between Socratic methodology, noted above. The two sets of dialogues present two different versions of Socrates. As the only fully surviving 'sources' for Socrates, it is impossible to weigh one against the other and to declare either more correct. The necessary conclusion is, instead, that Xenophon and Plato each depicted their former mentor according to their own plan. (And, indeed, while Xenophon's Socrates remains consistent, Plato's Socrates changes his interests, opinions and methodologies over the course of his author's career.)

The key to Xenophon's interest in resurrecting Socrates may be found in a common sentiment: namely, that the best route to learning is to find an expert in the relevant field. In *Memorabilia*, this is a lesson in progress when Hippias rudely interrupts Socrates and derides him for always saying the same things. The discussion of justice that follows (see above) is then an exemplification of the interrupted point that to learn about justice requires a qualified teacher (4.4.5). According to Xenophon, Socrates regularly acted upon the principle of seeking out specialists, when he led his pupils to those with knowledge that he himself lacks (4.7.1). Plus, Socrates' visit to Ischomachus is ascribed to his desire to learn by what means he sustains his reputation as *kalos kagathos* (*Oec.* 6.12–17). Furthermore, early in the *Symposium*, a similar proposition is made, with the help of some lines of verse credited to Theognis that crystallize the positive effects of associating with good men over bad. Hence, young Autolycus is encouraged to seek out a man whose lifestyle shows him able to teach *kalokagathia* (2.4–5; Theognis 35–6 W), increasing the humour in Lycon's closing praise of Socrates, noted above. Across Xenophon's dialogues, Socrates' demonstrated mastery of myriad fields of knowledge prerequisite to *kalokagathia* make him an ideal man to consult.

In this light, Xenophon's Socratic dialogues do more than simply defend Socrates by extolling his virtues and the positive benefits of his association. They also make such association possible through the proxy of the written text. Just as in the dramatic action of *Oeconomicus* Socrates brought his prior conversation with Ischomachus to Critobulus' attention, so, through his written recollection, Xenophon brings Socrates' discussion with Critobulus about household management to the reader. In this way, although departed, Socrates is able to continue his good work: for, 'The very recollection of him in absence brought no small good to his constant companions and followers' (*Mem.* 4.1.1). Thus, by remembering Socrates in writing, by reanimating the man whose association he considered to be of such benefit to his companions and bringing him to a wider audience, Xenophon undertakes his own public service.

Ghost in the machine

The utility that is established for the dead philosopher and perpetuated through the recollection of his conversations is also a hallmark of other reanimations. Thus, in *Hellenica*, amidst the uproar over the abandonment by Athenian generals of shipwrecked sailors at Arginusae on account of heavy weather (in 406 BC), Socrates is a voice of protest. When the council officers are pressed to put an illegal proposal to the assembly that would enable the generals' conviction without trial, Socrates is the only one to resist: for 'that man said he would never act in any way except in accordance with the law' (1.7.15). This represents a minor but significant intervention in a situation marked by corruption (Callixenus has been bribed to press the matter in the council; Socrates' fellow officers are intimidated into submission) and by rampant populism (with the mob demanding that the wishes of the People must be upheld). In practical terms, Socrates' defiance enables Euryptolemus to present the case for full and separate trials. It also puts Socrates on the right side. Before long, the people will soon repent of their decisions to reject Euryptolemus' proposal and to vote for the execution of the generals, bemoaning their deception and imprisoning the former advocates of this course (1.7.1–35). This biographical anecdote features also in *Memorabilia*, where adherence to his councillor's oath conveys Socrates' piety (1.1.18). Here, by contrast, his intervention contributes to the depiction of democratic Athens boiling out of control. However, sustaining *Memorabilia*'s apologetic agenda, *Hellenica* also makes Socrates a bulwark against injustice and a moderating force in Athenian civic life. Conversely, the Athenian citizens, a subset of whom will soon condemn Socrates to death, aggressively patrol their own privilege and are easily swayed towards illegal action and violence. The portrait works two ways.

   In this anecdote, the positive influence Socrates might have had is limited by the unreceptiveness of those around him. A more personal recollection offers a parallel scenario, during which a headstrong young Xenophon fails to heed Socrates' advice. Events are told in flashback at the very moment in the *Anabasis* when the character puts himself forward to become general (see Introduction and Chapter 1). On learning of the invitation from Proxenus to join Cyrus, Socrates warns Xenophon that the Athenians will be displeased, given the Persian prince's recent contribution to the Spartan war effort against their city. Thus, he recommends seeking divine guidance. Xenophon complies, but then poses the wrong question to Apollo, asking how he should reach them rather whether he should go, as Socrates had intended (3.1.5–8). The trials and tribulations that are about to unfold as the inexperienced new general struggles to bring the mercenaries home safely from Persia, plus the subsequent exile, might all have been avoided, had Xenophon followed his mentor's instruction. There is some ambivalence in this wistfulness, perhaps, for the journey is a formative experience for Xenophon, who (eventually) succeeds in bringing (most of) the Greeks (almost) home. However, by raising the spectre of 'what if', the author admits his youthful folly and exculpates Socrates from blame for the fallout.

The integration of Socrates' interventions into Athenian civic life and Xenophon's personal history thus continues the project of defending Socrates after his death, however quickly the historical narrative moves on. So too does the story of Tigranes' tutor in *Cyropaedia*, which brings Socrates back to life more obliquely. A sophist is first mentioned in the context of Tigranes' appeal that Cyrus allow his father to live despite his crime against the Median king Cyaxares (see Chapter 1). Cyrus had agreed to listen to this argument because he knew of Tigranes' admiration for the man (3.1.14). By implication, Tigranes' successful speech demonstrates his teacher's worth. However, it is the report of the sophist's execution that brings Socrates vividly to mind. First, according to Tigranes, his father's suspicion that the tutor was corrupting his son was the root cause; and second, in a final conversation before his execution, being *kalos kagathos*, the sophist advised Tigranes to forgive his father, because he committed wrongdoing through ignorance. Both the motivating factors and the sophists' measured acceptance of his demise resonate with Socrates' situation at Athens. Socrates is effectively written into Persian history in a transparent new guise. At the same time, the excuse that is awarded to the Armenian king, namely his jealousy at the higher esteem in which he believed his son held his teacher, provides a basis for Cyrus to spur Tigranes towards forgiveness. After all, his father's sins are only human (3.1.38–40). Through this hypothesis, Xenophon signals a possible explanation for the treatment of Socrates at the hands of angry Athenian fathers like Lycon and Meletus. Speaking through the character of Cyrus, moreover, the author transcends the usual parameters of defence to promote understanding and forgiveness on every side.

Again, this is a fleeting moment. However, the ghostly presence of Socrates in *Cyropaedia* provides a parallel for his evocation in spirit when ideas attributed by Xenophon to Socrates are reprised. To illustrate this, the theme of the 'dangers of beauty' is especially useful, because the relevant exchange in *Memorabilia* features a young Xenophon. Fitting the pattern of Socratic conversation sketched above, the mode is collaborative and the impetus is specific: Critobulus has kissed Alcibiades' son. For Socrates, this is a dangerous development. Seeking confirmation from Xenophon of Critobulus' transformation from a person of moderation and prudence into someone reckless and rash, Socrates proceeds to outline further negative consequences: namely, the willing enslavement of the kisser, their lavish spending on harmful pleasures and the loss of leisure time to devote to activities appropriate to *kaloi kagathoi*. Revealing himself to be up for just this sort of danger, the young Xenophon is initially somewhat sceptical at the power Socrates invests in a kiss, leading Socrates to chastise him twice over as a wretch and a fool. However, by contrast to the naïve resistance in *Anabasis*, this young Xenophon eventually takes the lesson on board, as evidenced by his elaboration that Erotes are called archers because they strike from a distance, a cap to Socrates' claim that a beautiful youth can inject madness from afar. As usual, the last word in the dramatized conversation is given to Socrates. Given the dangers, avoidance of beauty is the only possible strategy (1.3.8–13). However, in the written work the last word on the topic is uttered by the author Xenophon, who explains

Socrates' sexual continence through his practice of avoidance (1.3.18). In the context of *Memorabilia*, the episode exposes the thinking behind Socrates' conduct and, like every vignette, demonstrates his non-corruption of the young by showcasing the re-education of Xenophon.

The further incorporation of the theme seems to confirm the lesson as learned. The *Symposium* keeps it within a Socratic setting, where the dangers of kissing are raised in playful rebuke (once again) to Critobulus for his obsession with beautiful Clinias (4.24–6; by his name, this is likely the son of Alcibiades that Critobulus is chastized for kissing in *Memorabilia,* above). This time it is the crowning remark in a wider conversation during which Critobulus argues that beauty promotes virtue by making men more liberal with money, more fond of toil and of honour, more modest and more self-controlled (4.15). These radical claims are undermined somewhat by Critobulus' enthrallment to Clinias' beauty, which impels him constantly to search out Clinias and brings him physically to a standstill (4.12, 4.14, 22). Plus, they sit awkwardly with the pride Critobulus takes in achieving good things without enduring toil or danger or possessing wisdom, being beautiful himself (4.13). The discussion ends with Socrates describing how the 'bite' he felt after reading shoulder-to-shoulder with Critobulus passed after a few days (paralleling a comparison in *Memorabilia* between the effect of a kiss and a scorpion sting: 1.3.13), and a command that the beautiful young man stay away until he has started growing a beard (4.28). Clearly, despite ending on the same note, the conversation in *Symposium* is not a simple replay.

Rather, Socrates' teaching is combined into a series of episodes that cumulatively generate a wider discussion. The party itself begins with the elucidating spectacle of the adult symposiasts bewitched by young Autolycus' beauty, upon which basis the narrator declares beauty to be 'kingly' and his entranced lover Callias to be worth seeing

(1.9–10). Later, Socrates is thwarted in the attempt to rebrand his own ugly features as beautiful by the young dancers who give their vote to Critobulus (5.10, see above). Furthermore, the party ends when the kisses of the beautiful dancers inspire the audience, excepting Socrates, to seek such pleasures in their own marriage bed (9.5–7). For all Socrates demonstrates his resistance once more, and it is in this context that Lycon declares him to be *kalos kagathos* (see above), the playful tone defers any negative reading. In *Symposium*, Xenophon thus expands the argument, integrating Socrates' original teaching into a new interrogative framework that allows for a wider, more flexible and potentially positive evaluation of beauty.

Whether Xenophon directly received instruction from Socrates precisely as portrayed in *Memorabilia*, and whether Socrates truly participated in exactly this conversation at a real-life drinking party might be legitimately debated. Nonetheless, arguments that Xenophon attributes to Socrates provided the basis for the author's future thinking. Hence, the dangers of beauty and of kissing also inform the depiction of the Spartan and Persian kings in *Agesilaus* and *Cyropaedia*. So, Agesilaus' repeated refusal to kiss the beautiful Megabates, whom he passionately adores, is described as a triumph of moderation (*Ages.* 5.4). In the economy of praise (see Chapter 4), resistance to beauty is again worthy of praise. Indeed, Cyrus goes one step further by refusing even to look at the captive wife of Abradatas of Susa, lest he be distracted from his affairs by a longing to gaze upon her exceptional beauty (*Cyr.* 5.1.8). Thus, Cyrus specifically seeks to avoid the sort of debilitation exemplified by Critobulus whenever he catches sight of Clinias. Echoing Socrates, Cyrus then goes on to argue against his childhood friend Araspas that love is a form of slavery and not a free choice (5.1.9–12). Araspas initially laughs at Cyrus' caution. However, the theoretical point is then proven when, despite his protestations of imperviousness, Araspas falls in love with Panthea, whom he pursues aggressively to his own shame: an outcome that is greeted with Cyrus' knowing laughter (5.1.17; 6.1.31–7). In this episode of Persian history, which enables Cyrus to send the supposedly disgraced Araspas to spy on his enemies (6.1.38–41), the wise words of Cyrus and the dramatic trajectory are infused with a Socratic sensibility. At the same time, it might be noted that both Agesilaus and Cyrus are also credited with a 'Socratic' approach to hardy living and, like the subject of *Memorabilia*, offer positive models for imitation (for Cyrus see Chapter 1; on Socrates and Agesilaus, see Chapter 4). The teachings of Socrates, as Xenophon remembers or represents them, percolate through his writings, whilst Socrates' demonstrated virtues are re-inscribed in the bodily practices of Xenophon's royal subjects. The deceased philosopher is a spectral presence.

Conclusion

The memory of Socrates drives Xenophon's intellectual project. Marking his younger self out as a recipient of Socrates' advice, Xenophon's written re-enactments of the philosopher in action communicate the benefits of that prior association and replicate them for the reader. The collaborative conversations by which the philosopher offered practical lessons on morality and politics establish Socrates' credibility as a man of virtue and a public educator, countering the real-life accusations that resulted in his conviction and death. They also illuminate the nuts and bolts of Socrates' thinking, or perhaps more accurately package what Xenophon remembers – bearing in mind that this recollection is a conceit of the dialogues and so may or may not be accurate and may even be fabricated – into slices of Socratic wisdom for posthumous consumption. By reimagining Socrates' conversations, repeating and expanding and alternatively integrating details to forward specific interrogative agenda between conversations and across different texts,

Xenophon generates distinct philosophical perspectives. Even in the absence of his physical reincarnation, the permeation of tropes of representation and thought means that whenever Xenophon writes, Socrates is never far away (as the next two chapters will continue to show).

3

Rethinking the *Polis*

While the idea of the Greeks as a people unified by heritage and culture was well established by the end of the fifth century, Xenophon's Greece was made up of hundreds of autonomous communities called *poleis*, or in the singular *polis*, a word often translated as 'city' or 'city-state' (*politeia* means roughly constitution). Ranging in population size from a few thousand (the norm) to over 100,000 (Athens, an exception), these communities were not only clustered in and around the Aegean, but, following several centuries of sailing and settlement, they were spread around the Mediterranean too. Some were tied to others in networks of obligation, based upon geographical proximity or shared genealogy, or of domination and subordination, according to fluctuations in military power (as sketched in Xenophon's *Hellenica*: see Chapter 1). Nonetheless, each managed its internal affairs. In this, the key difference between *poleis* was where the power to deliberate and make decisions lay. The possibilities are neatly reflected in a scheme accorded by Xenophon to Socrates. As autocratic regimes, kingship and tyranny might be distinguished by their basis in consent and law *versus* the will of the ruler. Then again, under an aristocratic constitution officials are appointed to rule as commanded by convention, under a plutocracy it is those who meet the wealth requirements, and under democracy everyone qualifies (*Mem.* 4.6.12). The Greek *polis* could be governed in a number of ways: which was best?

This question became pressing in Xenophon's home town towards the end of the fifth century when Athens was losing the Peloponnesian War and proponents of oligarchy seized opportunities to reconfigure the democratic assembly and council by restricting the franchise, albeit with only temporary success (in 411 and 404/3: see Thucydides, *History* 8.53–98 and Xen. *Hell.* 2.3.1–43). Although Xenophon's status as a wealthy cavalryman has led to assumptions that he was anti-democratic and that he must have supported the oligarchic revolutionaries, his writings eschew this easy categorization. Instead, working through Socrates and his interlocutors (in *Memorabilia*) and authoring direct advice (in *Cavalry Commander*), Xenophon establishes a set of principles for the good citizen and the successful city that might apply within and beyond democratic Athens. Attainment of success is given greater consideration through examination of the Spartan way of life established by Lycurgus (in *Constitution of the Lacedaemonians*) and interrogation of tyranny (in *Hiero*), as well as the author's radical plans for reshaping Athens' economy (in *Poroi*). While Xenophon has no single blueprint for the well-run *polis*, his hypotheses on active citizenship, leadership, civic organization, economic activity and inter-*polis* relations suggest routes to good practice and prosperity.

Informed leadership and constructive citizenship

'What is a city?' 'What is a citizen?' (*Mem.* 1.1.16). On the surface, like the other questions by which Xenophon establishes Socrates' interest in human affairs (see Chapter 2), these seem rather abstract. Yet, when Socrates enters discussion over what makes a good citizen by inquiring about their core tasks (4.6.14), the answers which he delivers for consent amount to a programme of activity. Making the city richer and stronger, converting enemies into friends, and promoting harmony over conflict: to be a good citizen involves improving the city in matters of finance, war, foreign relations and public debate. The specific context for this instruction is a debate over whether the man praised by one speaker is a better citizen than one praised by Socrates. However, the underpinning principles of participation and enhancement also map closely onto the advice delivered to Charmides, son of Glaucon. Is not the man who refuses to 'grow' the *polis* and receive honour on this account a coward, Socrates asks, before asserting that Charmides, who answers with an ambivalent 'perhaps', is just this sort of man. After all, he is more capable in political affairs than current participants; and the mob, whom he shies away from addressing, is comprised of the most foolish and feeble individuals: leather-workers, carpenters, smiths, farmers and merchants, none of whom give thought to political matters. If Charmides were to deploy his existing talents in offering good advice and criticism in the assembly, it would be an advantage not only to other citizens, but to himself and his friends. The imperative is upon worthy and competent Charmides to exert himself to make the *polis* better (3.7.1–9). There may be some irony here, or alternatively wishful thinking, in that the historical Charmides went on to become one of the Ten that ruled from the Piraeus during the ruthless Spartan-sponsored oligarchy, and he died fighting the returning democrats in 404/3 (*Hell.* 2.4.19). Participation in politics did not work out so well. But, importantly, the role Socrates recommends to his talented young associate is one of active service.

Socrates' teachings on the city and citizenship thus align with his further interest in 'what is rule over men?' and 'what is a ruler of men?' (*Mem.* 1.1.16). The conversation with Charmides is one of a package in which Socrates advises Athenians who are either striving for or have been appointed to high office. The terms are familiar. Thus, for Glaucon, son of Ariston, who wants to command the city, the benefits extend from 'growing' the fatherland to fulfilling his own desires, helping friends, raising up his household and acquiring renown at home and abroad (3.6.2). Achieving this is dependent, however, upon learning everything about war, the city's defences, the silver mines and the grain supply, and upon developing skills of persuasion (3.6.3–18). The topics are wide-ranging, reflecting the immediate concerns of the city, but always education is essential. As Socrates later informs Euthydemus, 'command of the city, the greatest task of all, does not attend upon men of its own accord' (4.2.2). Hence, too, an unnamed aspiring general is sent for instruction to the self-proclaimed expert Dionysodorus, although in fact he receives better information from Socrates on his return (3.1.1–11). So does the new general Pericles, who admires Socrates for telling him what he needs to know and instructing him in these matters at the same time (3.5.21–4). With a focus on strategy and problem-solving as well as tactics, this is a very practical education. Of course, befitting the *Memorabilia's* apologetic agenda (see Chapter 2), these conversations establish Socrates as a good instructor. However, beneath these practical lessons lies a theoretical commitment to informed leadership.

In this model of constructive citizenship, the relationship between a leader and the city is one of mutual benefit. Conversely, poor leadership can foster a toxic environment. This, at least, is Socrates' explanation for the current condition of the Athenians, as described by Pericles. Both men agree that the *polis* and the Athenians have declined (3.5.13). Socrates at first suggests this is the result of having spent too much time at the top, and that it might be remedied were the Athenians to adopt the lifestyle of their ancestors, or to 'imitate' the lifestyle of those who are now preeminent (3.5.14; cf. 3.5.9–11). But for Pericles, who interprets the latter as a reference to the Spartans, the proposed journey towards *kalokagathia* (the virtue associated with being *kalos kagathos*, 'beautiful and good': see Chapters 2 and 4) is hindered by the Athenians' disdain for their elders and their lack of bodily care; a disobedience that arises from a celebrated contempt for rulers; an inability to work together to mutual advantage due to spite and envy; a preference for profiting from one another rather than being 'useful together'; and their distancing of themselves from common affairs, whilst also fighting over them (3.5.16). In their self-absorption, antagonism and isolation, these members of the *polis* are the antithesis of Socrates' constructive citizen, who is devoted to the public good.

Crucially, the targets of Pericles' vitriol are not the lowest citizens, the shipmen to whom Socrates accords obedience, but rather the hoplites and cavalrymen. Those who might be expected to exceed other citizens in *kalokagathia* are the 'most insubordinate' (3.5.19). As a result, no one in the army displays moderation, good order or obedience to authority. It is this condition that Socrates ascribes to rule by men who possess the least knowledge (3.5.21); and Socrates' own lessons to Pericles follows. A profound symbiosis is thus imagined between the leader and the city, where his competence dictates the character and conduct of the citizens, with consequences for the well-being of the *polis*. In the current circumstances, Pericles stands in great fear lest something terrible befall the city (3.5.1). Luckily, Socrates informs him, if he implements what he has learnt, good things will follow for everyone (3.5.28).

The practical advice Socrates offers to young men preparing for specific office in democratic Athens thus also conveys general principles for good governance. A conversation with the sophist Hippias provides a more direct model. In the process of establishing that 'what is lawful is just' (4.4.12), Socrates remarks, 'Do you not know that amongst rulers in cities those who are most able to make their citizens obey the laws are the best, and the city in which the citizens obey the laws above all carries on best in peace and is irresistible in war?' (4.4.15). And obedience to the law is achieved through concord, 'the greatest good to a *polis*' that is often encouraged by elders and the best men and by oaths: 'for when citizens abide by them, these cities are strongest and most prosperous; but without concord no *polis* will be governed well' (4.4.16). Earlier, Pericles had worried over the Athenians' lack of obedience and their inability to ever act in unity (3.5.20, 3.5.16). Now, Socrates makes these missing elements the foundations for success. Strikingly, in light of Pericles' lament that the Athenians will never revere the elderly nor train their bodies like the Spartans do (3.5.16), Socrates introduces his description by referring to Lycurgus the Spartan, who made Sparta exceptional by implementing obedience to the law (4.4.15). In the cross-over between Pericles' negative observations and Socrates' positive endorsements, it is possible to identify the bases for a productive society.

If there is any criticism of Athenian democracy within Xenophon's *Memorabilia*, it is subtly conveyed. Comments are restricted to the ignorance of the assembly and its leaders, and to a rather damning portrait of one portion of the citizen body, a portion that is roughly equivalent to those who embarked upon oligarchic enterprises in 411 and 404/3. Socrates in fact found himself in conflict with both the democratic assembly and the Thirty. As president of the assembly, he opposed the impromptu vote to execute the Arginusae generals as illegal (1.1.18, see Chapter 2; for events in 406, see *Hell.* 1.7.1–35, by which account Pericles is one of the condemned). In addition, he raised the ire of the oligarchs by criticizing their murderous programme on the grounds that it was a poor leader who reduced and worsened the citizen body (1.2.32; for Critias' conduct, see Chapter 1). These are telling moments of resistance considering the importance Xenophon's Socrates sets on 'growing' the city and on obedience to the law. However, in both cases it is certain behaviour in specific contexts that provokes opposition. In *Memorabilia*, neither Socrates nor his interlocutors offer a structural critique against any specific form of *politeia*. At most, one might infer that the city of Athens would benefit from possessing better leaders and being more like Sparta.

Likewise, in *Cavalry Commander*, a self-standing treatise that expands upon Socrates' conversation with a new appointee on the best way to approach the role (*Mem.* 3.3.1–5), Xenophon confines his advice to the current political environment. From observations and recommendations posed, this is one in which cavalry numbers are deteriorating (*Hipp.* 1.2, 9.3), tensions exist between the Council and cavalry (1.8) and individual citizens shirk their responsibilities by buying themselves out of cavalry service (9.5). These developments suggest underlying difficulties in a city that may still be suspicious of the loyalty of its horsemen, following their implication in the oligarchy of 404/3, and where wealthy citizens are not playing their expected part in a democracy dependent upon liturgical and military service. Rather than address structural issues, however, Xenophon delivers detailed instructions to the cavalry commander that will maximize the competence of his force and reinvigorate the cavalry. These include practical measures the commander must take to recruit, condition and train cavalrymen, lieutenants and their horses (§§1–2), plus the responsibilities, qualities, manoeuvres and tactics that the commander must demonstrate during civic displays and in the field (§§3–9). In essence, Xenophon provides the cavalry commander with the knowledge necessary to become an informed leader. 'To read these things a few times will suffice', he writes (9.1). At the same time, by advising the Council to regulate the training and recruitment of horses (1.8), to commission a cavalry unit populated by resident foreigners to defray costs, bolter numbers and foster rivalry (9.3–6), and to attach a troop of motivated infantrymen to it (9.7), Xenophon works within the system to improve it.

A similar agenda may underlie Xenophon's works *On Hunting* and *On Horsemanship*. Providing technical instruction covering the use of horses to capture prey, and caring for and training horses, respectively, these are almost antecedents to *Cavalry Commander*, with its focus on managing horse and men. Like *Cavalry Commander*, which makes a strong cavalry and a capable commander essential to Athens' defence (7.2–4), both works anticipate their readers' military contributions.

In addition to readying the young hunter to serve the state (see Chapter 4), *On Hunting* explicitly commends the application of hunting skills to warfare (*Cyn.* 12.1), while *On Horsemanship* contains the underlying assumption that a horse is purchased for war (*Eq.* 3.7, 11.13). These three separate works might thus be considered a triptych, through which the author cultivates the next generation in their civic responsibilities, oriented around military participation and leadership. In this way, much like Socrates conversing with the young, Xenophon is a constructive citizen.

Law and order in a surveillance society

By contrast to this practical focus on political participation, Xenophon's *Constitution of the Lacedaemonians* presents a structural critique. Echoing Socrates in *Memorabilia*, it launches with notions of Spartan superiority and exceptionalism, wondering how the most sparsely populated of cities could also be the 'most powerful' and 'most well-known'. An explanation is found in the way of life established by Lycurgus (1.1). In the account that follows, the style and consequences of Lycurgus' laws are sketched, starting from a point of difference: 'For that man did not imitate other cities, but by discerning the opposite in relation to the majority, provisioned his country with prosperity' (1.2). Building outward from principles introduced by characters in the *Memorabilia*, Xenophon sketches Spartan customs in their own terms and by comparison to those of other Greeks as well. The result is an extended analysis of a polity of superlative qualities that conforms to no other, but which others might profitably emulate.

The breadth of Xenophon's discussion reflects the scope assigned to Lycurgus' laws. Regulations cover the production of children (§2), the education of boys through to manhood (§§3–4), the establishment of public messes (§5), the sharing of authority, property and food (§6), prohibitions on financial undertakings (§7), obedience to the laws and its oversight (§8), measures to promote a good death over a shameful life (§9) and a commitment to virtue (§10), military organization on manoeuvres and in camp (§§11–12), the role of the king in war (§13) and the relationship between the king and the community (§15). At every stage, the benefits are articulated. For example, physical exercise for women, secretive liaisons and the sharing of wives produce strong off-spring (1.4, 5, 10). Strict punishment, physical hardship, a restricted diet, survival through thievery and submission to adult authority foster in boys modesty and obedience, resilience and resourcefulness and respect for rulers (2.2, 7, 11). Enforced labour, backed up by corporal punishment, discourages insolence in youths, whilst being compelled to walk in silence and head-down instils a sense of shame (3.2–4). Finally, for those reaching their prime, conflict through competition leads individuals to pursue *andragathia*, the quality associated with being an *anêr agathos*, a 'good man', and to become most powerful, so that each will commit their strength to aid the city (4.3, 4.5). Through a combination of exposition and elucidation, Xenophon describes a Spartan life course marked by tight social controls designed to harden citizens and ensure their sublimation to the needs and will of the state.

As the language of excellence suggests, there is a strong moral dimension to Lycurgus' laws. One the one hand, undesirable conduct is discouraged through prohibition and structural constraints. So, paralleling Persian drinking practices (see *Cyropaedia*, Chapter 1), Lycurgus organizes public dining in ways that limit the consumption of food and drink 'which overpowers the mind and body' (*Lac. Pol.* 5.4). Moreover, equal distributions and living conditions eliminate grasping after money and a life of luxury (7.3). On the other hand, commendable behaviour is promoted through a combination of punishment and enforcement. Hence, sanctions against proven cowards encourage virtue on the battlefield as a route to a beautiful death or glory (9.1–2); and the requirement to compete in elections to serve as Ephor ensures the maintenance of *kalokagathia* into old age (10.1). Indeed, punishments are meted out on those who do not attempt to be their 'best', helping to enforce the compulsion upon each Spartan to practice every virtue that made *kalokagathia* central to the Spartan way of life (10.4). Citizenship is dependent upon fulfilment of this (10.7). Thus, by Xenophon's account, Lycurgus' laws aim above all at a creating a moral citizen.

At a civic level, Xenophon's Sparta maintains itself through a series of power relationships that cut across the generations and the citizen population. Women, whose primary role is to produce children (1.4), remain entirely outside this scheme. Boys, however, first found themselves subject to a supervisor (2.2), whose instruction and punishments were devolved to the wider citizenry in his absence (2.10); and by implication on adulthood they too would advance into these roles. Later in life, they might be elected to the Council of Elders, the good men responsible for trials concerning matters of life and death (10.1–2). Supporting this order were the ephors, whose fuller executive powers permitted them to fine and demand immediate payment from whomever they wished and to remove magistrates from office with instant effect (9.3–4). One circumstance meriting their attention is presented: when a sparring partner refuses to obey instructions from an overseer to cease a fight, the supervisor will ask the ephors to impose a fine, to dissuade the offender from disobeying the law (4.6). Such strategies of coercion are further supported by mechanisms of social control and exclusion. The man seen to visit his wife invites shame (1.5), while whoever walks home drunk from the public messes may be excluded from dining in future (4.7). The same fate awaits the proven coward, who is additionally prohibited from wrestling, joining festival choruses and getting married; the women in his family cannot wed either. In addition, he must give way in the streets, and, under threat of violence, avoid wandering around at his ease, as though he were irreproachable. Death is preferable to dishonour, Xenophon remarks (9.4–6). Indeed, for the recognized coward who foregoes this solution, the consequence is a kind of social death. Relegated to the bottom of the pecking order, barred from participation in shared activities and denied the opportunity to continue his family line, he is effectively expelled from the community. In Sparta, citizens police one another. The consequences for individuals found to deviate from the community norms are profound.

The success of the Lycurgan way of life thus lies not only in the cultivation of men 'inclined towards the good of the *polis*' (4.1), but in the creation of a system that incentivizes adherence to its strictures, or perhaps more accurately dis-incentivizes dissent. As Xenophon notes up front, Spartan prosperity results from obedience to Lycurgus' laws (1.2). This is secured by two further mechanisms. First, by consulting Delphi, Lycurgus won endorsement from Apollo, making any disobedience of the divinely sanctioned laws an act of sacrilege (8.5). Second, he initiated a compact between the king and the *polis*, which Xenophon implicitly connects to the longevity of the Spartan *politeia* over a period when other constitutions have changed (15.1; a very long time indeed, given that Lycurgus was reportedly a contemporary of the sons of Heracles: his laws are of 'greatest antiquity', 10.8). Key here are the ephors and the king, or in fact two kings (the plural is used at 15.4–5). As observed already, the former effectively operated as an independent authority, possessing carte blanche to punish misdemeanours. However, the ephors also had military duties (4.3, 11.2, 13.5); and they represented the *polis* in a monthly exchange of oaths with the king (15.7). The king was distinguished from other Spartans by a series of privileges – receiving choice cuts of sacrificial meat, a public mess tent and additional food to distribute as honours –, and through his special function as intermediary with the gods on behalf of the city (15.2–5). In war, his role was that of priest and general (15.11). Thus, he performed sacrifices to launch campaigns and before issuing orders for the day; and although he did not manage every minutiae on campaign (13.10–11), he led the marching army (13.6), decided when and where to camp, dealt with matters arising (13.10), and entered battle at the front of the first division (13.6–7). The king was thus head of state, and in war he possessed executive powers. However, under the terms of the oath, he too was constrained: his promise to rule as king according to the established laws was met with a commitment from the ephors to support him as long as he continued to do so (15.7). In effect, the power of the ephors to punish offences against the law extended to the king. At Sparta, everyone was invested in the maintenance of law and order: from ordinary citizens to councillors and magistrates to ephors and kings.

In sum, Xenophon's *Constitution of the Lacedaemonians* describes an integrated and self-perpetuating socio-political system. Its author's positive evaluation is evident in the praise awarded to Lycurgus, a man 'at the peak of wisdom' (1.2), in the encouragement of doubters to examine the evidence for themselves (1.10. 2.14), and in his amazement that no other city has chosen to adopt the Spartan way of life and reap the benefits for itself (10.8). In fact, broadly shared (except regarding pederasty, at 3.12) and unremittingly presented as opposite to Spartan practices, the lifestyle choices of other Greeks emerge badly. Sometimes, the criticism is explicit. Nutritional neglect and a sedentary life of wool-working for girls, plus the untrammelled copulation of husbands and wives, are not conducive to producing strong offspring (1.3–5). Then again, dining at home is a great source of laxity and recklessness (5.2), and shame is absent when the company at dinner are of a similar age (5.5). The detriment of these customs to the strength and moral fibre of the citizen body are clear. Elsewhere, however, condemnation is implicit. In other cities, boys are indulged: they are given the best education and schooled in letters, music and wrestling, and they have sandals to soften their feet, many clothes, and as much food as they like (2.1). Citizens relax their physical training, even though they still undertake military service (4.7). Each father alone controls his children and servants and property (6.1). Men make as much money as they can through farming, trade and crafts (7.1). Powerful men show no fear towards magistrates (8.2). In each instance, the critique emerges through the benefits brought by Lycurgus' reverse measures: the lifelong training that fosters endurance and readiness; the sharing of power between fathers to ensure fair treatment of sons (6.2); the dedication of citizens to being useful rather than making money (7.4); and the observation and promotion of obedience (8.2). By explaining Lycurgus' logic, which really means extrapolating his intentions by imagining the advantages of organizing the Spartan polity in the ascribed fashion, Xenophon establishes the superiority of the Spartan system, and infers what is wrong with the weak-bodied, soft-living, pleasure-seeking, family-abusing, money-loving, authority-snooking Greeks.

The *Constitution of the Lacedaemonians* thus presents a holistic scheme, wherein the model of Spartan excellence is sustained through its declared merits and through a comparative prism that disparages other ways of living. On this basis, Xenophon's *laconophilia*, or 'love of Sparta', has frequently been read. After all, Xenophon served with the Spartan army under Agesilaus II, and he settled in the Peloponnese, presumably under that king's patronage. There are reports that he even sent his sons to be educated at Sparta (Plutarch, *Agesilaus* 20.2; Diogenes Laertius 2.6.54). However, towards the end of the treatise, Xenophon makes an important qualification. Stating initially that 'if someone were to ask whether it seems to me that even now the laws of Lycurgus remain unchanged, by Zeus I could not say this in full confidence'. Then, contrasting the former reticence of the Spartans with their recent ventures to seek wealth and power overseas, Xenophon concludes 'they clearly obey neither the god nor the laws of Lycurgus' (*Lac. Pol.* 14.1–7). The location of this observation (§14) has merited some confusion, for unlike the parallel debunking of the Persian king Cyrus' successors in the *Cyropaedia* (see Chapter 1), it is not placed right at the end, but rather immediately before the closing section on the ephors and kings, which begins with a statement of continuity in government. Even if this is the result of a scribal error, the clashing sentiments still beg an explanation. This might be found in a change of heart: perhaps the negative comments are a late addition that reflects Xenophon's disillusionment with Sparta following the series of overweening acts narrated in *Hellenica* (see Chapter 1).

And yet, the accusations against Sparta fit a longer pattern of behaviour. Instead of living at home on modest means as before, Spartans now travel abroad, setting themselves up as governors; corrupted by flatterers, they seek fortune and power; and instead of other Greeks requesting their leadership in thwarting injustices, they seek to prevent the return of their rule (*Lac. Pol.* 14.2–6). Framed through a series of temporal divides between 'then' and 'now', such behaviours might reach back into the fifth century, to the Persian Wars (the renegade regent Pausanias at Byzantium: see Thucydides, *History* 1.128–34) and on through the Peloponnesian War (the general Lysander, who received gifts and cult worship at cities freed from Athens on the Asia Minor seaboard, and Gylippus, who stole the spoils from the defeated city: Plutarch, *Lysander* 16–18). Meanwhile, the final proviso could fit any moment from the Corinthian War (395–386 BC) onwards. Where earlier the city was drawn in contrast to other Greek *poleis*, Sparta 'now' is opposite to its former self. In this way, sustained praise descends into pointed criticism. But the terms are important: for it is not the laws of Lycurgus that are at said to be at fault, but the Spartans who fail to follow them. Notably, Xenophon does not directly take the logical next step in the argument: that if the laws are not observed, then the *politeia*, which is supposedly geared to maintaining them, is flawed. Nonetheless, the jarring intervention disrupts the prior logic and thereby invites the question of whether the corrupting pressures are exclusively external.

Happy tyrants make happy cities

Where the well-being of Athens and Sparta depend, in different ways, upon their citizens' positive participation, under tyranny the prosperity of the city depends upon the disposition of its ruler. This is the premise that emerges through the dialogue between Hiero, tyrant of Syracuse (ruling 478–466 BC), and Simonides, the elegiac poet. *Hiero* opens as an interrogation of the pleasures experienced by the tyrant by contrast to a private citizen, and ends with the poet revealing the means by which he might achieve happiness, 'the most beautiful and blessed possession known to humankind' (*Hiero* 11.15). In developing this approach, Xenophon utilizes the figure of the happy tyrant, familiar to Plato's *Republic*, and echoes Isocrates' concern with what makes a good king in his letters to Nicocles, the ruler of Cyprus (Isocrates *Letters* 2, 3 and 9). However, the execution is uniquely Xenophon's. Constituting yet another imagined encounter set in the past ('then', 1.1) and between persons long deceased, *Hiero* reworks a longer literary-philosophical tradition that sets a wise man in conversation with a ruler at his court into a format akin to his Socratic dialogues. A further frame might be found in Xenophon's *Hellenica*, where tyranny is associated repeatedly with injustice (see Chapter 1), especially in light of Hiero's self-excoriation over the fact that a tyrant 'lives day and night like one condemned by the judgment of all men to die for his wrongdoings' (7.9–10). However, the *Oeconomicus* also ends with an assessment by Ischomachus to Socrates that the ability to command willing men is a gift from the gods to those that possess moderation, whereas tyranny over the unwilling is a reward for men who lead their lives so that, like Tantalus, they remain in perpetual fear of dying twice over (21.12). Matching this, death is Hiero's constant fear. It is in resolving this fear that Simonides provides a solution to the tyrant's deficit in pleasure and his surfeit of pain (*Hiero* 1.2). A series of short measures that also direct the tyrant away from injustice will transform the polity into willing subjects.

Key to Simonides' proposal is the cultivation of affection between the tyrant and his subjects through measures that benefit the wider community. After all, it is their presumed antagonism that lies at the root of Hiero's negative appraisal of the tyrant's life. For on the one hand, the tyrant lives in constant fear, to the extent that he constrains his movements (1.11–12), he is permanently on guard against attack (2.9–11, 18; 4.11; 6.7–8), he eliminates the best of citizens who might oppose him (5.1–2), and he even worries over the loyalty of his hired guards (6.11). On the other, his pleasures are ruined because praise may be false (1.15), love may be feigned (1.29–38), friendship may hide contempt (3.8–9, 6.12–13) and honours are forced (7.7). Indeed, fear is not only a source of pain, but corrupts every pleasure (6.6). As Hiero reveals, his response to the dilemmas raised by these anxieties lead him to murder conspirators (2.17); to rob temples and men to meet the exaggerated needs brought about by sustained threat (4.11); and to remove men whose qualities threaten the status quo, so that only inferior men are available for service (5.1–2). Tyranny thus perpetuates itself, by compelling the tyrant to actions that will incite hatred and burden the populace (8.8–10), whilst the perpetrator cannot make up the deficit that all the wrongdoings bring (7.12). Through Simonides' probing and Hiero's responses, Xenophon describes a political system that undermines the sort of positive goals for good leadership set out in *Memorabilia*. Trapped in a downwards spiral of never-ending abuse, every action undertaken by the tyrant to secure his position diminishes the body politic. Not only is the tyrant unhappy, but the populace exists at an unsteady tension point between suppression and revolt.

The solutions offered by Xenophon's Simonides moderate the relationship between the tyrant and his subjects. First, to earn thanks rather than enmity, a ruler must devolve the issuing of punishments onto other people, whilst maintaining his responsibility for distributing prizes (9.1–11). This is an adaptation of the imperative to reward and punish that Cyrus identifies and implements in *Cyropaedia*, and it combines another principle witnessed in Cyrus' camp and at Sparta: that competition and prizes inspire soldiers towards military excellence (1.6.18, 20; see Chapter 1 and above). In *Hiero*, the end-goal is greater economic industry. For such small investment, Simonides promises great returns: a boost to agricultural production and growth in revenues and commercial activities, plus an increase in moderation amongst the busy citizens. Winning the gratitude of the people and teaching them what is best go hand in hand. Furthermore, putting the mercenaries at the service of the city with the purpose of extending protection, bearing the brunt in battle, intimidating neighbours into peace, and punishing wrong doers will make residents willing to pay for their upkeep (10.1–8). Finally, Hiero should use his private property for the public good: beautifying the city, outfitting the citizenry with armour, creating employment opportunities, supplying horses to win victories at festivals and thus competing with other heads of states. As a result, Hiero's subjects will feel friendly towards him and everyone will sing of his virtue. By further consequence, the tyrant will be able to travel freely and receive friendship and adoration, obedience, support and wealth, all willingly supplied (11.1–15). Give and you will receive – to friends, the city, allies – might be Simonides' motto. The poet thus proposes a transformation in behaviour by the tyrant that will also transform the city, creating a new equilibrium founded upon reciprocity and willing obedience. Although the dialogue ends appropriately with a promise of blessed happiness to Hiero, with improvements to everyone's circumstances and morality, the benefits run two ways. To return to

Oeconomicus, by following Simonides' instructions, the new Hiero will be like the ruler blessed by gods. No longer ruled by fear, in effect he is no longer a tyrant.

Towards peacetime prosperity

Whether filtered through staged conversations or articulated through a carefully contrived exemplar, Xenophon's interrogation of the *polis* so far remains at an abstract level. Readers may be primed for action, but the advice is of general applicability. By contrast, the examination of 'revenues' or 'resources' or 'ways and means', as the title of the *Poroi* might be translated, aims at resolving a particular political-economic crisis. This arose in the aftermath of the Social War (357–355 BC) between Athens and disgruntled members of the Second Athenian Confederacy, which ended in a truce mediated by the Carian king Mausolus that established the autonomy of Cos, Chios and Rhodes, the major complainants. According to Xenophon, the conflict was devastating to Athens' public purse (5.12). The *Poroi* responds to this situation. Stimulated by the argument from Athens' leaders that the poverty of the masses causes the city to act unjustly towards other cities, Xenophon proposes measures to increase the city's wealth and thereby eliminate the Greeks' suspicions (1.1). Delivering recommendations in the first person, and speaking to a communal 'we', Xenophon rethinks elements of Athens' socio-economic organization and its relationship with other *poleis*. Although addressing the Athenians in writing, rather than in person before the assembly, Xenophon thus acts like a good Socratic leader, proposing measures to 'grow' the city: to improve Athens' wealth, security, reputation and power.

The methods recommended by Xenophon are striking in their apparent modernity. Most notably, with the ambition to increase revenue, trade and industry, he appears to subscribe to the goal of economic growth, one of the defining principles of capitalism. However, the ways in which this is to be achieved are distinctive to the immediate socio-political environment. Classical Athens was a stratified society, and divisions by wealth and status are reflected in the different measures proposed. In this respect, it is worth noting that the overall purpose is to generate enough income for the citizen body to maintain itself through the redistribution of state funds (1.1; 4.33). Although some of the regulations below seek to harness private individuals' desire for wealth, the needs of the People are the driving motivation for enhanced economic activity. Only when they are well-supported will men devote themselves fully to their training and military duties; only then will the city be 'more obedient', 'better organized', and 'more successful in war' (4.51–2). Xenophon thus promotes a welfare system of the sort modern capitalists decry. He also argues for it in terms that are the opposite to the neo-conservative equation between dependency upon the state and slothfulness today. Nor, though, is he driven by socialist sentiments or empathy for his fellow man. From a pragmatic perspective, human nature makes support for the poor essential to the well-being of the *polis*.

In the pursuit of income to fund this project, attention quickly turns to Athens' metics (*metoikoi*). These are people who 'live with' the Athenians, although they originate from elsewhere. Xenophon describes Lydians, Phrygians, Syrians and 'barbarians of all different sorts' making up the majority (3.4), although historically their number included Greeks from other cities too. Crucially, metics are not entitled to state benefits and they pay a special tax (2.1). The challenge, then, is to maximize their fiscal contribution. To this end, Xenophon suggests a series of incentives to improve their disposition towards the city and to increase their overall numbers. This includes removing the requirement for infantry service, which is dangerous and takes metics away from their businesses; awarding them the privilege of riding with the elite cavalry (cf. *Cavalry Commander* 9.6); transferring empty housing lots into their ownership (metics cannot otherwise own property); and setting up a system that awards honours to appointed guardians for expanding the metic community, in the expectation that these awards will attract many more stateless folk to Athens (2.2–7). In this model, foreign residents' commitment to the city is exchanged for the removal of onerous duties, extended rights and visible markers of special status.

An understanding that individuals might be motivated to act in desirable ways by promising personal gain also underpins Xenophon's ideas for the marketplace. Prizes are suggested for officials who resolve disputes fairly and efficiently and thereby facilitate a quick turnaround for trading ships, thus increasing the volume of trade (3.3). In addition, the promise of profits and honours – front-row seats in the theatre and hospitality – to merchants and ship-owners who prove themselves useful to the city will provide a basis for friendship (3.4). The increased number of settlers and new arrivals that result from these measures will in turn boost economic activity and produce higher income through sales, rents and custom dues (3.5). Ultimately, the expansion of trade brings a proliferation of opportunities for the state to accumulate wealth. Furthermore, the same combination of incentives might encourage private investment in state ventures that build upon the potential offered by marketplace expansion, be it creating infrastructure to support increased activity at the port of Piraeus or launching a state-owned merchant fleet. High returns are promised to citizens who invest in a capital fund; and the permanent inscription of their name in a roll of benefactors would surely inspire foreigners, cities, kings, tyrants and satraps all to join (3.6–14). Xenophon invites the Athenians to look beyond their city and to implement one of his favoured strategies for good leadership: rewarding friends for past service to secure future advantage through a mutually beneficial relationship (as discussed in Chapters 1).

For the slaves who are key to Xenophon's next economic proposal, there are no such benefits. Silver is a valuable and much-desired trading commodity (3.2, 4.5–10), and for Xenophon the mines are not only a divine gift that is unique to Athens (1.5), but also an endless reservoir of wealth (4.11). Extraction of this valuable metal is limited only by the availability of manpower (4.33). The first step, then, is for the state to build that manpower base (4.17–22). Eventually numbering three slaves for every citizen (4.18), the expanded workforce could be hired out to local and foreign privateers (4.12, 22). Through such rentals massive sums would be realized for reinvestment and expenditure (4.23–4). Furthermore, in order to encourage venture mining, each of Athens' ten tribes could be given slaves to work new shafts on speculation, with the spoils evenly shared between them. Far from generating conflict, the combination of private and state-run operations will maximize discovery and extraction (4.31–2). Xenophon is aware of some potential drawbacks in this scheme: the problem with recruiting when there is a surplus of labour (4.22), the difficulty of accruing the capital necessary for initial investment (4.34), and the possibility of overworking the mines (4.39). The answer is to match the number of workers to the work required, and to take a scaled approach to investment, starting with an affordable outlay (4.37, 40). Finally, as for the envisaged expansion of trade, increased industry will require the development of new infrastructures. Knock-on benefits will include taxes and rents from state-owned houses and furnaces, following the settlement of such a large population in what will effectively become a new city (4.49–50; cf. 4.40).

This is an ambitious plan. As for his ideas about trading, with their focus on market expansion and investment, Xenophon's thinking on the silver mines seems familiar. In the pursuit of wealth through the exploitation of natural resources, (unfree) human resources are to be deployed, investment and returns are weighed up, and strategies are developed to manage risk. However, the facilitating role of the state in developing a 'nationalized' (slave) labour force and the unquestioning commitment to maintenance for citizens that run across the *Poroi* again warn against anachronistic readings of Xenophon as some kind of proto-capitalist. Rather, working within the existing socio-political and economic framework, Xenophon identifies the basic mechanisms by which revenue is produced, and considers how to improve them. The answer is always to go bigger: accrue more taxes, extend trading and investment opportunities, and make fuller use of available resources. In the expanded Athens, with its increased population and newly developed urban centres, there is a role for citizens, metics, foreigners and slaves. Although Athenians will be the primary beneficiaries of the resulting wealth, there are advantages for at least some of those who make it happen.

The anticipated contributions from self-interested individuals and communities beyond the *polis*, however, raises a vital precondition for Xenophon's ambitions, namely peace. While Xenophon is keen to establish that the outbreak of war would not disrupt his plans for mining (4.40–8), nonetheless it is only with the continuing cessation of conflict that merchants and traders, rich men ready to invest, craftsmen, teachers, philosophers, poets and their patrons, and sightseers will flock to Athens (5.3–4). The arguments presented here speak to a very live debate over Athens' future following the Social War. Calling upon history to promote co-operation over coercion, Xenophon proposes interventions to reconcile and unite the Greeks through dedication to peace on land and sea (5.5–10). Athens will thereby earn the favour of their allies and avoid the crippling costs of war that have been felt so recently (5.11–12). While its terms remain general and the tone is aspirational, this is a very targeted set of advice that chimes with a pamphlet written by the rhetorician Isocrates *On the Peace*, and with the policy associated with Eubulus, who, from measures taken to organize the harbour agency in the mid-to-late 350s, seems to have shared some of Xenophon's economic principles.

It also answers the problem of the Greeks' relentless self-immolation in *Hellenica* (see Chapter 1). If his measures are adopted, Xenophon promises that the *polis* will be safe and prosperous (6.1). The opening dilemma, that the poverty of the masses causes Athens to treat the allies unjustly, has been resolved. So, then, might the city itself become more just: 'For I have always believed that of whatever sort its leaders are, so will become the *politeia*' (1.1). With its foremost men freed now to act justly, citizens will follow. There is a moral benefit to be had too. Furthermore, with money in hand, a rebuilding of the city – its temples, walls and dockyards – will be accompanied by a return to the priests, council, archons and cavalry of their 'ancestral rights' (*ta patria*). In the utopian future, the Athenians will enact a return to the past. Here, at last, might be some oligarchic sentiment: an echo of the calls for the restoration of to the 'ancestral constitution' (*ho patrios nomos*) familiar to fifth-century plotters. However, fundamental here is not any ideological principle, but the creation of a utopian city in which everyone has their dues: the poor are well fed and the rich are saved from financial burdens. In the new Athens conjured by the *Poroi*, mutual participation in economic activity leads to all-round improvement and harmony.

Conclusion

In his political thinking, Xenophon appears less interested in promoting any one form of constitution and more in establishing operational parameters for success. What on the surface appear to be theoretical discussions reveal a series of practical measures that will contribute towards a city's prosperity, power and fame. First, across the board, establishing a productive relationship between different elements within the city is key. This is articulated in advice to Athens' future leaders and to the tyrant of Syracuse to align their personal ambitions and activities to the public good (to 'growing' the city), which in Hiero's new world includes motivating citizens towards the same goal. In Sparta, mutual dependency is already built into the system, where social conventions and legal prescriptions ideally constrain everyone in their prescribed role. A similar dynamic is encouraged by the allocation of discrete roles to citizens, metics, foreign traders and slaves as part of the *Poroi*'s cumulative project to improve Athens' revenue. Benefit is shared and sustained through joint endeavour. This principle also informs Xenophon's equine triptych, by which readers are primed for future action in service to the city. Second, obedience to the law, or at least the avoidance of injustice, is also promoted. Again imbedded at Sparta, the former is recommended by Socrates as a pre-requisite for harmony at home and strength abroad, while without it Hiero and Athens are at risk from internal and external enemies, respectively. The well-run *polis* is thus governed by moral principles.

4

Living a Good Life

In the world of Greek epic poetry, the good (*agathos*) man combined physical prowess with high status and wealth. Virtue (*aretê*) was the sum of these qualities, expressed through victory in combat trials and athletic contests and confirmed by the award of prizes and honour and the achievement of fame. Being good was thus a matter of possessing power and position, above and beyond men of lesser skill and resources. Out in the historical world, in didactic poems sung at drinking parties, the same vocabulary denoted distinction. However, reflecting the texture of the social life of elite symposiasts, being good also meant conducting oneself in the right sort of way. Praise (and blame) acquired a moral dimension. At the same time, political fluctuations meant that men born to wealth and power, who might have described themselves as 'the good' (*hoi agathoi*), witnessed those they considered to be socially and morally inferior ('the bad', *hoi kakoi*) usurping their status and authority. This is reflected, for example, in the contortions that the late-fifth-century author of the *Constitution of the Athenians* (once spuriously identified as Xenophon) must undertake to explain how the Athenian democracy sustains itself, despite being governed by the worst sort of people. Such perplexity amongst Athens' disempowered elite was likely exacerbated by the state's appropriation of the standard terminology to praise its benefactors: such as the 'good man' (*anêr agathos*) Thrasybulus of Calydon who was honoured for the murder of Phrynichus in the fight-back against the oligarchs in 411/10 BC (Meiggs and Lewis, *Greek Historical Inscriptions* 85). In such a topsy-turvy world, where social and political boundaries were blurred and fluid, what distinguished a good person from the bad? How might one live a good life?

This, of course, was the Athens of Xenophon's youth, and if his recollections of Socrates' instruction in human affairs are taken at face value, then these may have been questions that directly occupied him at the time. Returning to the theme in his written work, Xenophon developed a coherent vision of desirable personal qualities as well as their opposites. In this scheme, virtue was expressed by individuals in their treatment of other people, as appropriate to their political or social role. In addition, virtue could be taught. Whilst Xenophon continued to utilize the traditional terminology and military excellence remained a possible route to virtue, by establishing a clear moral line and broadening opportunity, he radically transformed what it might mean to be good and to live well. In the process, his own work became a stepping-stone towards the attainment of a good life.

Virtue *vs.* vice

To some degree, both questions – what? and how? – are answered in the person of Socrates. As observed in Chapter 2, the *Memorabilia* in its entirety is dedicated to demonstrating Socrates' ability to improve his young companions. The exemplarity of his character is the basis for this. Being most self-controlled (*enkratestatos*) in his passions and appetites and most capable of enduring (*karterikôtatos*) winter and heat and every toil (*pantas ponous*), he eliminates lack of self-control and softness in matters of sex and toil (*aphrodisiôn akrateis, pros to ponein malakous*) in his associates and makes them eager for virtue (*aretês*). Under his guidance, they apply themselves to becoming 'beautiful and good' (*kalos kagathos*), with Socrates himself as a model for imitation (1.2.1–3). By this account, Socrates literally embodies virtue: for the qualities attributed to him are grounded in an exertion of will over his corporeal desires and somatic responses. To contemplate Socrates is to thus understand virtue; to imitate him is to approach it.

The value of the model that Socrates represents is demonstrated further in targeted discussions that weigh it favourably against the alternatives. As someone who approached the matters of eating, drinking, sex, sleeping, heat and cold with extreme incontinence (*akolastoterôs*) – the areas in which Socrates conversely exerted restraint – Aristippus stood in special need of such instruction (2.1.1). The conversation initially proceeds in the typical question and answer fashion, with Aristippus duly admitting Socrates' point that only the self-controlled are capable of ruling (2.1.7). However, the lesson is thwarted by Aristippus' lack of interest in becoming such a person: 'Indeed, I situate myself alongside those who wish to spend their life in greatest ease and pleasure' (2.1.8–9). Hence, Socrates changes tack by demonstrating that those who rule have a more pleasurable existence. By this evaluation, willing endurance of hardship and toil brings enjoyment, as well as praise and envy, whether in the hunt or in the pursuit of friendship or the harming of enemies, or in service to home, friends and fatherland. Ultimately, 'efforts sustained through endurance (*karterias*) result in deeds that are beautiful and good (*tôn kalôn kai kagathôn ergon*)' (2.1.18–20). Pleasure in accomplishment and public recognition is elevated beyond the gratification of bodily desires.

To convince Aristippus of this proposition, Socrates cites several good men (*hoi andres agathoi*) as authorities. Of these, Prodicus' display speech 'On Heracles' is most elaborated, with divine personifications of Virtue (*Aretê*) and Vice (*Kakia*) each attempting to persuade a youthful Heracles that they offer a route to happiness. A key distinction between their two approaches is the matter of toil. For Vice, the pleasures of the table and bed may be achieved with the very least effort (*aponôtata*): 'fear not that I shall lead you into labouring (*to ponounta*) and hard work to provide these things' (2.1.24–5). For Virtue, by contrast, toil and diligence (*ponou kai epimeleias*) are essential if benefits are to be achieved: winning divine favour, the affection of friends, honour from the city and admiration from the Greeks all require prior effort (2.1.28). Recalling Prodicus' words enables Socrates to draw a contrast between two different modes of life, where vice is marked by the sensuous indulgences resisted by the virtuous. He thereby presents Aristippus with the same choice as Heracles: between immediate gratification of the body and the delayed joy that accompanies public acclaim.

Through this exchange, virtue is defined in a positivistic fashion by reference to underpinning qualities and through a set of oppositions that intimate what it is not. Viewed from both directions, virtue, like vice, is essentially a set of attitudes oriented around the self that are expressed in ways of living. The basic principles are reiterated in the conversation between Socrates and Euthydemus around self-control (*enkrateias*). Prefaced by familiar assertions of Socrates' personal practice and endorsement of it as useful in the pursuit of virtue (*aretê*), the end point is again a reframing of pleasure, this time specifically studying and attending to what is beautiful and good (*ti kalon kai agathon*), managing one's body, organizing the household, and making oneself useful to friends and the city (4.5.1–2, 4.5.9–10). However, the interim debate extends the model by making freedom, wisdom and moderation correlate with self-control, and counter to its opposite. Through this equation, lack of self-control (*akrasia*) leads invariably to an inability to correctly distinguish what is good from what is bad, and therefore also results in wrong choices (4.5.3–8). In this framework, the man who lacks self-control is comparable to a slave – obedient to the worst of masters – and to the stupidest of animals (4.5.5, 11). It is not simply the case 'that the man who yields to bodily pleasures has nothing whatsoever to do with any form of virtue (*oudemias aretês*)', as Euthydemus concludes. Rather, as

Socrates adds, 'only the self-controlled are able to contemplate the most important matters and, separating them by type according to word and deed, to choose the good (*agatha*) and reject the bad (*kakôn*)' (4.5.11). To embrace a life of incontinence is to become trapped in a network of lowered autonomy and detrimental decision-making. By contrast, self-control combines the sort of qualities that foster learning and enable the right kinds of choices. It is a stimulus to virtuous action and pleasurable living, newly defined.

Personal morality and public service

The project to which Xenophon's Socrates dedicates himself in *Memorabilia* is a persuasive one: to convince the young men of Athens to devote themselves to a life of virtue. However, sitting around chatting with Socrates, or indeed reading Xenophon's compilation of Socratic conversations, will only take you so far. In order to move from theory to practice, what youngsters need is training in the field. This is the argument that underpins Xenophon's treatise *On Hunting*. Although the work is dominated by technical instruction for the pursuit of wild animals, covering the use of dogs and the instruments and strategies suitable for capturing different creatures, it is bookended by demonstrations of the wider benefits of this activity. From the first, hunting offers a means to 'become good (*agathoi*) in war and in other matters from which fine (*kalôs*) thought, word and action are compelled to come' (1.18). A group of young men schooled by the centaur Chiron who were each of noted virtue (*aretên*) offers proof (1.5–17). The one thing they share is esteem, the tokens of which include divine favour, immortality, a propitious marriage and public renown. For each mythological individual, the root of their virtue is briefly given. Sometimes it is a matter of personal qualities: a love of toil (Meilanion, Menestheus); virtue (Nestor); piety (Aeneas) combined with moderation (Hippolytus); wisdom (Palamedes); and skill in craftsmanship, speaking and war (Machaon and Podaleirius). Military achievement is also frequently lauded. Strikingly, many of these accomplishments explicitly or implicitly benefit others. Thus, Theseus destroyed the enemies of Greece and strengthened his fatherland; Odysseus and Diomedes brought about the destruction of Troy; and Antilochus sacrificed himself to save his father. At the same time, other helpful acts are singled out: Aeneas rescuing his family's gods and his father, and Asclepius curing the sick. This aspect is reinforced by Xenophon's closing remark that whenever any city or king or Greece itself needed help, these men provided it (1.17). As for Socrates' young associates in *Memorabilia*, the virtue and fame of Chiron's pupils lie in service to the community.

This is the end goal too for Xenophon's readers. In practical terms, learning to hunt involves developing skills that have military application, such as endurance in marching, carrying arms, sleeping and guard duty, following orders, pursuing the enemy and saving allies in flight (12.1–5). However, as the closing sections of *On Hunting* make clear, the physical and mental training that such toils (*ponoi*) involve also effects a moral improvement, making men moderate and just and committed to the truth. The hunter's enthusiasm for virtue is demonstrated through vigilance towards injustice and suffering in the city and its hinterland. Hunting is thus the one pleasure that need not be avoided; and it is a source of 'good (*agathoi*) soldiers and generals' (12.8–9). There are echoes of *Memorabilia* in both the conception and the outcome. However, with such directed assertions, Xenophon seems on the defensive. Pre-empting possible arguments, he brands potential naysayers ignorant and jealous, and makes their dissent further evidence of the value of the recommended education (12.10–12). The sort of man who indulges in wicked pleasures, who speaks foolishly – i.e. against men trained in hunting – and so acts to the disadvantage of family and friends because he cannot distinguish wrongdoing will never be employed to save the city (12.13). Such men will disobey 'laws and good words (*agathois logois*)', and, having never learned through toil what a good man ought to be, they will be neither pious nor wise (12.16). The educated man, by contrast, will look after his household to the further benefit of the city (2.10–11); he will obey the laws and talk about and listen to matters of justice, and attend to the city's safety (12.14–15). The distinction between the educated and uneducated, those who hunt and those who do not, is thus exemplified in a personal morality grounded in virtue (love of toil) or vice (love of pleasure) that reveals itself through detrimental or beneficial actions within the domestic and public spheres.

The trained hunter effectively becomes a good citizen, measured by his commitment to the common good. Such an outcome is possible because hunting imbeds personal qualities that promote actions and attitudes that transfer over into civic life. This is emphasized in the intertwined character sketches that follow upon a closing warning not to envy men who pursue personal advantage. This type of person steals from individuals and the city, is useless when it comes to the safety of the community and possesses a body that is weak and ill-favoured for war (13.11). Hunters, by comparison, will surrender their bodies and property to the common good. Attacking animals rather than friends, hunters in fact becomes better and wiser (*beltious . . . sophôteroi*), because the end goal is so difficult to achieve: a great love of toil and strength (*philoponiai, kratêsêi*) are vital to success (13.12–14). Such fundamental differences in ability and acumen are accompanied by differences in tolerance for bad behaviour (*kakoêtheias*) and profitmongering; voices which are 'ugly' (*aischran*) or 'fine' (*euepê*); and neglect of or devotion to the gods (13.15–17). With impacts upon the body and behaviour, the improvements afforded by hunting are holistic. So too are the benefits, which are imbedded in Xenophon's promise to young readers that by following his recommendations they will be favoured by the gods and by pious men: and so 'they might be good (*agathoi*) to their parents, their own entire city, and to every single citizen and friend' (13.17).

With this full circle back to the opening exempla, where the accomplishments of Chiron's pupils were described in just such terms, *On Hunting* reaffirms its own scheme. Furthermore, by promising this outcome directly to young readers the author awards his own work a place in the educational process. As Xenophon states, in an aggressive pre-emptive attack against sophists who might criticize his writing (and whose work, he complains, focuses on trivial affairs and delivers 'empty pleasures' that fail to inspire virtue), his own work aims to make wise men good (*sophous kai agathos*) and to therefore be of permanent utility (13.6–7). Thus, life in the wild prepares today's generation of would-be heroes to contribute productively to the well-being of their city. And, as a conduit for necessary knowledge and a stimulus to virtue, so does Xenophon's treatise *On Hunting*.

Best of the Greeks

The understanding of virtue as a personal quality expressed in action is exemplified further in Xenophon's portrait of the Spartan king Agesilaus II. Written as an encomium, or praise speech, after the death of its subject (10.3), *Agesilaus* bears witness to his virtue. To this end, Xenophon first narrates the king's deeds in order to illustrate his manner, and then turns to examining 'the virtue (*aretên*) in his soul', again evidencing this through specific actions (1.6, 3.1). The resulting composition both describes the man and defines virtue. Hence, Xenophon's portrait has an educational component. For, 'the virtue of Agesilaus is a model for those wishing to practice manly excellence (*andragathia*). For who, imitating a man who is pious, becomes impious (*theosebê, anosios*), or just unjust (*dikaion, adikos*), or moderate insolent (*sôphrona, hybristês*), or self-controlled lacking in control (*enkratê, akratês*)?' The oppositions line up as proof not just to Agesilaus' character but to the qualities that might be achieved by following the example of a man who 'brought every virtue to his citizens' (10.2). As for Cyrus in the *Cyropaedia* and Socrates in *Memorabilia*, the opportunities for imitation and self-improvement formerly available in real life are extended to Xenophon's present-day readers through his quasi-biographical profile.

Presented in summary, the qualities ascribed to Agesilaus correspond closely to those recommended to Socrates' interlocutors (see above). Their fuller testimony through events directly involving Agesilaus or the daily routine of his life, moreover, makes these qualities relational. Agesilaus' piety is exemplified by his treatment of the Persians Spithridates and Pharnabazus, each of whom he receives and treats fairly under oath (3.2–5). His justice and self-control with regards to money is proven by the generosity of his own distributions and the willingness of others to offer donations, whenever he needed money to do some good for the city or a friend (4.1–6). Resistance to pleasure is shown in sharing portions and enduring physical hardships along with his soldiers, and in the refusal to kiss beautiful young Megabates, who he ardently desires (5.1–5: see Chapter 2). In each case, Agesilaus' virtue is established through his treatment of others, whether enemies, associates, or subordinates. Then again, other people are also engaged in the process by witnessing Agesilaus' actions, recognizing particularly the moderation with which he comports himself in temples and public places (5.7). Or in battle, where he demonstrates courage (*andreia*) in the front ranks, his own battered body, as much as the victory trophy that offers 'an everlasting memorial to his virtue', allows observers to make their judgement on his soul (6.2). Indeed, this is exactly how the *Agesilaus* works: as a compilation of activities that comprise a lasting reminder of the king's excellence. The text thus solidifies Agesilaus' reported belief that actions-as-memorial were more appropriate to his achievements and to a good man than a sculpted statue (11.7). Re-embodied in Xenophon's account of his deeds, the man in all his virtue is simultaneously remembered and offered once more for (positive) evaluation.

As well as corresponding each virtue to a particular action in a specific setting in a more systematic fashion, *Agesilaus* thus widens the scope of beneficiaries beyond the civic realm imagined in *On Hunting*. Agesilaus' virtue is layered and directed towards outcomes within his zone of operation. Hence, many of the described deeds involve war and diplomacy, as befits Agesilaus' status as king: a position he was reportedly granted on account of his virtue (*aretêi*) as well as his birth (1.5). Some of the described activities map clearly onto the qualities later afforded to Agesilaus. On entering Asia with a force of Spartans and allies, for example, the action deemed to be 'his first noble (*kalon*) accomplishment' (1.12) is the preservation of an armistice with Tissaphernes, even after the Phrygian satrap had broken his oath. However, other qualities and accomplishments align him with other good Xenophontic leaders, and especially the Persian king Cyrus (in *Cyropaedia*: see Chapter 1). Thus, after surprising Tissaphernes by attacking and pillaging cities in Phrygia (1.15), an action deemed to be 'worthy of a general' (*stratêgikon*), Agesilaus cleverly (*phronimôs*) created opportunities to enrich his friends (1.17–19), and won over his enemies by kindness (*priotêti*) as well as force (1.20–2). Acting admirably (*agastôs*), he corralled a cavalry from conquered Phyrgians (1.23–4), and then instituted training and competitions (1.25–7), before heading out to victory in the battlefield (1.28–32). Whilst these actions conform to Xenophon's broader understanding of good practice in leadership, their consequences are specific. Marching with his army and sacking the territory around Sardis, Agesilaus restores honour, wealth, freedom and stability to the Greeks in the region (1.33–5, 37–8).

Furthermore, when instructed by Sparta to return home, Agesilaus set aside his newfound fame and power and his ambitions to conquer

Persia. Obedient to the fatherland and acting to help the state, he chose the nobility and justice (*ta kala kai dikaia*) that came with danger over easy profits: a decision that makes him 'worthy of admiration' (*axion agasthai*) (1.36). This moral coding emphasizes the rightness of Agesilaus actions; and indeed 'love of his city' (*philopolis*) and obedience are later added to the suite of virtues resident in his soul: 'for he believed the work of a good king was to do as much good as possible for his subjects' (7.1). What is more, this ethic extended to his treatment of the Greeks: for as a philhellene, he lamented the reduction of Corinth at Spartan hands (7.4–5), and even while he was fighting other Greeks, he looked to their common good (*koinou agathou*) by making trouble (*kakon poiêsôn*) for the barbarians (7.7). In short, Agesilaus' virtue remains constant, while the beneficiaries of his services change according to the immediate context.

This role-specific element is emphasized in a pointed set of polarities that set Agesilaus favourably against the Persian king. Paralleling earlier comments on the justice of the Spartan king in relation to money, a comparison is drawn between Agesilaus' minimalist domestic arrangements and the Persian king's intertwined desires for gold and silver and world domination. The juxtaposition of Spartan simplicity and Persian wealth is an old trope, familiar from Herodotus (*Histories* 9.82). However, the moral extends twice over. First, because Agesilaus' expenditure does not exceed his income, there is no impetus to behave unjustly (*adikon*). Second, in Xenophon's opinion, the nobility involved in fortressing oneself against an enemy is surpassed by making one's soul unassailable by money or pleasures or fear. A further comparison between the efforts that the two kings made to satisfy their needs for food, drink and sleep extends the point. Where thousands busy themselves in procuring pleasures for the Persian and readying his bed, the Spartan, being a man enamoured by toil (*philoponos*), takes pleasure in consuming whatever comes to hand, and he can sleep anywhere (9.2–3; cf. 5.2). Thus, Agesilaus leads the happier life, surrounded by good cheer (*euphrosynais*). Finally, still on the topic of lifestyle, being unable to endure the heat or cold the Persian king mimics the weakest of wild animals (*asthenestatôn thêriôn*); coping without trouble (see his endurance of summer sun and winter cold and his toiling in adversity at 5.3), the Spartan king, by inference, acts like the good man that his Persian antithesis does not.

The driving lesson here is that wealth does not make a ruler good, an assessment accredited directly to Agesilaus. Instead, it is 'whoever is himself better (*ameinôn*) and leads the better people (*ameinonôn*)' (8.4), or the man most loved by the city, with the most and best friends, who shows himself superior in benefitting the father land and his companions and in punishing enemies (9.7). The latter qualifications follow Agesilaus' dismissal of victory in chariot racing as an indicator of *andragathia* (9.6). Instead, these are the tokens of victory in 'the most noble and magnificent competition', which bring the greatest renown in life and death (9.7). As a man who excels in exactly these terms, Agesilaus is the real victor, shortly to be declared by Xenophon 'a good man in every way' (*anêr agathos pantelôs*) (10.1). Or alternatively, given the direction and energy of his actions, plus the excellence of his soul, Agesilaus demonstrates the truth of his own maxim: that it is not easy living that befits kingship, but 'beauty and goodness' (*kalokagathia*) (11.6).

To create a portrait of virtue, *Agesilaus* combines narrative depiction, complemented by alleged character motivation and belief, with direct authorial comment signalling the author's admiration or characterizing his subject's accomplishment. The result is a holistic and coherent depiction of the best kind of king, which in its tenets reflect the wider rubric for 'virtue' and for leadership encountered in Xenophon's other works. This is sustained even when Xenophon appears to be on the back foot, presenting something that might be argued only to counter it. For example, Xenophon deflects the possible charge that the small size of the army Agesilaus brought to Boeotia means that he could seem to be praising Agesilaus for leading his men into serious danger by stating his admiration for Agesilaus in presenting an army equal to the enemy: a result of the training and inspiration offered by the king (2.7–8). This is evidenced in the colourful description of troops rushing into battle at Coronea (possibly including Xenophon amongst them: see Introduction), and again elided when Agesilaus shows bravery (*andreion*), risking his life and meeting injury in a frontal assault (*Ages.* 2.9–13; cf. *Hell.* 4.3.19–20). Or Sparta's future failings – as sketched in detail in *Hellenica*, these include major defeats in the field, loss of territory and an assault on the city itself – are simply raised so that Agesilaus' responsibility can be denied. Tellingly, in the very next anecdote, set immediately after the battle of Leuctra, Agesilaus is leading the Lacedaemonians on a ravaging expedition to avenge the murder of their friends by an enemy coalition (2.23). Xenophon knows that different stories may be told. However, his response is to paper over the gaps with self-authored justifications and further examples of virtuous conduct that sustain the threatened model. As the Spartan king successfully navigates the historical terrain, everything supports the initial description of Agesilaus as 'the perfect *anêr agathos*' (1.1).

Virtues for all

Across *Memorabilia*, *On Hunting* and *Agesilaus*, virtue is at once multifaceted and constant. The qualities that Socrates attempts to inculcate in his young associates are also those fostered in trainee hunters and displayed by Agesilaus, with variation and direction appropriate to their individual circumstances. As discussed so far, a good life, which is both the expression of virtue and a source of pleasure, would appear to be the preserve of men of wealth and status. However, the very final lines of *On Hunting* shake up this assumption: 'For not only have the sort of men who loved hunting become good, but also the women to whom the goddess gave these things, Atlanta and Procris and the others' (13.18). These are the mythological huntresses favoured by Artemis, female equivalents to Chiron's novices. While Xenophon fails to specify how their goodness reveals itself – an intriguing question in light of the fact the civic model recommended to young readers implicitly maps onto contemporary male roles – the notion that virtue might cross the gender divide suggests that excellence is possible for everyone.

A similar appreciation is evident also in *Cyropaedia*, where ordinary Persians are given the opportunity to fight in close combat with the elite *homotimoi* ('men of equal honour') on the grounds of their shared potential. Nurtured on the same land, and with bodies and souls that are in no way inferior (*ouden cheirona, ouden kakionas*), Cyrus informs his soldiers, these men lack only the leisure required for education, because they must earn a living. Once they are similarly armed with a corselet, a shield, and a short or double-edged sword, these soldiers might become 'beautiful and good' (*kalon kagathon*) and of equal worth, striving for victories and the advantages that they bring (2.1.15–17). The validity of this proposition is sustained in the repeated success of Cyrus' highly trained forces in battle.

It is also manifest in the person of Pheraulas. Introduced as 'a Persian of the People' (*Persês tôn dêmotôn*) whom Cyrus already esteemed for being 'not ignoble in his body and soul', Pheralus initially encourages his fellow soldiers to enter Cyrus' competition for virtue (*aretê*), accepting the principle that anyone might show strength in the face of the enemy and seize concomitant rewards (2.3.7–16). Later, towards the end of *Cyropaedia*, it transpires that he has benefitted from Cyrus' open-minded strategy and received his own rewards. The context here is a quip by Cyrus that if Sacas were to throw a clod of earth he would easily hit a good man (*anêr agathos*): the joke is that instead of hitting one of Cyrus' friends close by, Sacas' missile strikes Pheraulas, who is riding past on a mission for the king. By now, thanks to Cyrus' largess, Pheraulas is a rich man. However, Pheraulas finds his riches a burden. Thus, he happily transfers their management and enjoyment to Sacas. The moment is significant: for Cyrus has just delegated the day-to-day running of his empire so that he might have leisure to devote himself to his friends (*Cyr.* 7.5.42–5). This is exactly what Pheraulas now does. While Sacas takes over ownership and the associated responsibilities for redistribution, Pheraulas will dedicate himself to Cyrus' service and to caring for his friends. In the process, Pheraulas makes himself and his friend Sacas happy. In his new life, this good man of the people – the son of a farm labourer who had left formal education to work his father's fields (8.3.31) – not only fulfils the potential Cyrus identifies for every man, but even mirrors the efforts of the Persian king, whose virtue everyone should imitate (see Chapter 1). By Pheraulas' own measure, he lives the best possible life, doing what brings him pleasure (8.3.45–50). Like the common soldiers who make the transition to the higher ranks, Pheraulas' upward mobility results from a combination of innate qualities and opportunity.

The *Oeconomicus* is more circumspect in its ascription of aptitude for virtue across humankind, and yet more revolutionary in some of its precepts. The second half of the dialogue comprises the recollection by Socrates of a conversation with Ischomachus, whom everyone regards as 'a beautiful and good man' (*kalos kagathos anêr*, 6.12), as a means of illustrating practical measures for success in estate management to the ambitious young Critobulus (see Chapter 2). Initially, this conversation focuses on Ischomachus' role in training servile members of his household to perform their duties diligently. The terms for choosing a female housekeeper and male overseer and the focus of their instruction are remarkably similar. The former is selected for being the most self-controlled (*enkratestatê*) in relation to eating, drinking wine, sleeping and men, while lack of control (*akrateis*) concerning wine and sleep and a tendency to fall in love are to be avoided in the latter (9.11, 12.11–14). Loyalty (*eunoikôs echein, to eunoein*) is taught in both cases by offering a share in success (9.12, 12.5–7). In addition, the housekeeper is taught justice (*dikaiosynê*) through being shown that greater honour, freedom and wealth come to the just over the unjust (9.13). For the overseer, diligence (*epimelê*) is induced through the same promise of profit and honour (12.15–16), whilst for male household slaves more widely behaving justly is a route towards praise, wealth 'as if he were free (*eleuetherois*)' and honour 'as if he were beautiful and good (*kalous kagathous*)' (14.9). Implicitly, not every individual will show the necessary virtues nor be ready for instruction. However, on principle women and men share propensities; they possess the same ability to be receive instruction; and they are granted parallel motivations and rewards. Moreover, these same individuals are slaves. The intended endpoint of this line of thinking may be the slaves' accommodation to their unfree status and circumstances: a familiar control technique. But importantly, within this model, slaves are recognized as moral agents.

The underlying assumption that human beings share the same operating code also informs the training that Ischomachus offers to his impressionable young wife. Certainly, by his argument, there are differences between the genders: the body and soul of a man is more capable of endurance than a woman's, and where men possess greater courage, women are more fearful. However, god grants memory (*mnêmên*) and diligence (*epimeleian*) and self-control (*enkrateis*; cf. 7.6) to both. The divine design that suits men and women to different roles in the household readies them to accomplish good things within their natural field of activity by consequence of the same underpinning virtues (7.23–8). This nuancing of the gender boundaries is strengthened by the metaphors that Ischomachus deploys to direct his wife's running of the household. Paralleling her efforts to those individuals who bring order to a dancing chorus, an army, a trireme and a merchant ship, Ischomachus also recommends that his wife behaves, variously, like the 'leader of the bees', the 'guardian of the laws', a garrison commander and a queen (7.32–8; 9.14–15). The skills of organization and leadership required for the woman in the home are essentially those required in the men's world. Socrates gets the point when he declares, 'By Hera, Ischomachus, you show your wife has a masculine mind (*andrikên tên dianoian*)' (10.1). Although the wife's accomplishments appropriately remain firmly within the female domain – it is here that she will earn honour from her husband and increase good things (*ta kala te kagatha*) through virtuous living (*dia tas aretas eis ton bion*) (7.42–3) – her masculine aptitude blurs the gender divide.

A woman's capacity to learn even forms the basis for a set of jokes in Xenophon's *Symposium*. At several points during Callias' party, a group of hired entertainers (again, by inference, slaves) become the focus of his guests' attention and their conversation. On their first appearance, a dancing girl juggles twelve hoops to the accompaniment of the pipes, before jumping in and out of a circle formed by swords. Each time, Socrates concludes that women can be taught. The first trick provides evidence that 'a woman's nature happens to be no worse than a man's, though needing reason (*gnômês*) and strength (*ischuos*)' (2.9). So, like Ischomachus in *Oeconomicus*, the symposiasts might confidently teach their wives whatever branch of knowledge they want her to know. To this proposition the symposiasts are initially sceptical, given Socrates' own track record in training his difficult wife: a fact Socrates acknowledges and humorously flips by making the education of his wife a matter of training in his desire to get on with other people. The second trick, performed with boldness and conviction, leads to a broader point on the teachability of *andreia*, or courage, which, given its most literal translation as 'manliness', should be a gender-specific quality. This time, Antisthenes jokes that the dancer's trainer might advertise his abilities to the Athenians and teach them to dare (*tolman*) the enemy spears just as, Socrates had noted, the dancing girl dares (*tolmêrôs*) the sword. The jester Philip then identifies Peisander as someone who would specially merit this education, conjuring an image of the cowardly demagogue tumbling between knives (2.8–14). The male citizen can learn qualities for war from the female dancer. Befitting the sympotic occasion, the banter is playful, but the discussion follows on from a more seriously posed debate over whether 'beauty and goodness' (*kalokagathia*) might be taught, and if so, from whom (2.2–7: see Chapter 2). Strikingly, too, the claims follow the logic of Socrates in *Memorabilia*, when he makes *andreia*, and other similar qualities, a matter of variation between individuals, but also something that can grow through learning and effort (3.9.1–2). Why not also a woman, *Symposium* asks? The dancer's performances sustain the underlying point that virtues can be learned, and more specifically that women may be educated even in attributes associated with men.

Conclusion

The virtues that Ischomachus imagines to be shared between men and women, as well as between masters and slaves, are notably the same as those attributed to and recommended by Socrates, fostered amongst young hunters, and displayed by Agesilaus. Self-control, continence, moderation, and courage are qualities possessed and demonstrated by the 'good' person, in tandem (variously) with justice, piety and diligence. Not everyone has the opportunity to become virtuous. However, with the right sort of training (physical, educational) and aided by right kind of intermediary – be it the boys' philosopher, the hunting tutor, the commoner's king, the slaves' master and mistress, the wife's husband, the performer's instructor – anyone might embark upon a journey towards virtue. For the citizen or king, this might lead towards public service; or for the slave or the wife to benefitting the household. To live a good life means to improve the lives of others. This is Xenophon's stated aim in the treatise *On Hunting*, and arguably it underpins all his work. Through the presentation of models for imitation, wise conversation and direct instruction, the writer makes himself useful. Thanks to his industry, anyone can embark upon better living through Xenophon.

5

Thinking through Xenophon

When Xenophon wished that his work *On Hunting* would prove useful and remain unrefuted 'for all time' (13.7), he could not possibly have predicted the depth, diversity and persistence of engagement with his writings over the next two thousand-plus years. In some respects, his fortunes have been tied to wider cultural changes and trends in intellectual life that have driven the popularity of ancient Greek writers for extended periods of time. That this book exists today is due to a continuing academic commitment to understanding the Classical world that took shape in the nineteenth century, as a concentration of trends in education and thought that stretched backwards to the Enlightenment and Renaissance. These in turn would not have been possible without the preservation of Greek texts at Byzantium following the collapse of the Roman Empire. And this happened only because of a sustained and vibrant engagement with ancient Greek authors under Rome. For every ancient author, the route between then and now was never guaranteed. However, Xenophon was considered important enough for his works to be copied, and fortunate that those copies survived the vagaries of destruction and decomposition to be rewritten and preserved. In addition, while in outline similar stories of transmission from classical antiquity to the present day can be told for many surviving authors, the significance of Xenophon's works and future patterns of engagement with them were determined by their specific contents, form and style. Xenophon's generically diverse, past-oriented and philosophically inclined investigations into politics and morality – a thinking through of human affairs – offered opportunities for successive generations to orient their own investigations: to think about themselves and their world through Xenophon.

Moving forward in time, this chapter illustrates the dynamics of this interaction. Rather than aim for completion, it draws upon examples that highlight how later writers made use of Xenophon's works by integrating them into their own philosophical and theoretical inquiries and modelling themselves upon Xenophon and his historical characters. Different examples could be given, and alternative trends could be sketched. However, attending to specific moments in Xenophon's reception history and the immediate intellectual, political and/or social context permits an intimate understanding of Xenophon's shifting fortunes and the bases for his continuing utility.

Integration

The Roman politician, orator and philosopher Marcus Tullius Cicero (106–43 BC) offers a good place to start. Cicero's translation of Xenophon's *Oeconomicus* into Latin at the age of twenty may have been exceptional (see *On Duties* 2.87). However, his immersion in Greek literature corresponds to an ever-growing preference for a Greek education amongst members of Rome's ruling elite. Conquests in the eastern Mediterranean during the Late Republic brought physical copies of Greek texts along with teachers to Rome and opened opportunities for schooling in Greek cities. That Xenophon was part of the general educational package is suggested by Cicero's letters to friends and family as an adult. For example, writing to Atticus in 60 BC regarding advice about windows from an architect called Cyrus, Cicero quips 'you find fault with the education of Cyrus (*cyropaedia*)'. By displaying and assuming knowledge, Cicero reveals the friends' shared familiarity with Xenophon's work (*Letters to Atticus* 2.3).

Advice to his brother Quintus on his reappointment as proconsul to Asia in 59 BC proceeds on a similar assumption. Here, however, the reference to *Cyropaedia* is integrated into an argument around leadership. Urging his brother towards self-restraint, Cicero adds that if he continues to master his desires, Quintus might appear to local Greeks as if he has stepped out of the annals of history (*Letters to Quintus* 1.1.7). Exactly which historical person Cicero has in mind starts to become clear when he introduces the importance of governing the multitudes of Asia in a mild fashion (*lenitas*: equivalent to the Greek *praotês* attributed to Cyrus when he shows mercy to the Armenian king) in order to promote willing obedience (~ Xen. *Cyr* 3.1.41, 1.1.5):

> Only a really great man, gentle by nature and cultivated by instruction and devotion to the highest pursuits, can so behave himself in a position of such power that those under his rule desire no other power than his. Such a one was Cyrus as described by Xenophon, not according to historical truth but as the pattern of a just ruler; in him that philosopher created a matchless blend of firmness and courtesy.
>
> Cicero, *Letters to Quintus* 1.1.22–3, tr. Shackleton Bailey

The conundrum faced by Quintus is that faced by Cyrus, and the solution provided by Cicero is explicitly Xenophon's. With the further recollection that the victorious general Scipio Africanus always carried a copy of *Cyropaedia* (cf. Cicero, *Tusculan Disputations* 2.26.62), the principles expounded in the work for the Persian king are endorsed for the real-life Roman governor. The next invocation to attend to the happiness of subjects, as well as their basic needs, also recalls Xenophon's *Hiero* (*Letters to Quintus* 1.1.24, 27; see Chapter 3). However, it is *Cyropaedia* that offers the stated model for rulership. Thus, almost ten years later, acting as Proconsul in Cilicia, Cicero can confidently reassure Paetus of his own competence as general: after all, he has worn out his copy of *Cyropaedia* entirely (*Letters to Friends* 9.25.1). Cicero thus incorporates Xenophon's writings into his argumentation and understanding of leadership. In the context of his own life story, this allegedly involves their practical appropriation and implementation within the context of Roman provincial governance.

More widely, Xenophon's different texts offers a surfeit of ideas which can be integrated into new hypotheses. Whether Cicero is seeking proof in the experiences of Xenophon and the advice of Socrates for the efficacy of dreams and oracles, or endorsing Theramenes' sanguine approach to death, or arguing for the pleasure of a simple diet, Xenophon is a valuable resource (*On Divination* 1.25.52, 1.56.122 ~ Xen. *An.* 3.1.5–8, 11–14; *Tusculan Disputations* 1.40.96 ~ Xen. *Hell.* 2.3.56; *Tusculan Disputations* 5.35.99; *On Ends* 2.92 ~ Xen. *Cyr.* 1.2.8). This is true also for Cato the Elder, as reimagined by Cicero. *On Old Age* is a quasi-Socratic conversation set in the recent past between the notable statesman Cato and his young contemporaries, Scipio and Laelius. One on occasion, Cato partially appropriates the drinking pattern set by Socrates in stated preference for 'cups, like those described in Xenophon's *Symposium*, that are small in size' to describe how old age has reduced his appetite (*On Old Age* 14.46 ~ Xen. *Symp.* 2.26). Cato also excerpts passages from the deathbed speech of Cyrus as a preliminary to his own elaborations on the topics of bodily vigour in old age and the immortality of the soul. In this last instance, Cato is aided by 'reason and argument', plus 'the renown and authority of philosophers of the highest tier' (*On Old Age* 8.30, 21.77 ~ Xen. *Cyr.* 8.7.6, 17–22). Within the conceit of this dialogue, Xenophon's works automatically belong to the Greek literature that Cicero asserts have contributed to Cato's unexpected erudition (*On Old Age* 1.3). As such, they are a basis for the understanding conveyed by the character on his author's behalf.

Xenophon is thus an aid to Cicero's own philosophizing. Whilst retaining authority in their new settings, extracted fragments of Xenophon's works facilitate his line of thinking (as do excerpts from other Greek authors, it should be said). Moreover, Cicero raises criticism. In *Brutus*, a dialogue on Roman oratory in which Cicero is the principle speaker, it is stated that everyone is reading 'the life and training of Cyrus'. Yet, despite this work being 'assuredly brilliant', this development is not a good thing. For it means that the personal accounts of Romans like Marcus Scaurus and Quintus Catulus – the latter composed 'in pleasant Xenophontic style' – are being ignored. Xenophon's encomia may be 'useful' as a model for autobiography, but *Cyropaedia* is 'not appropriate to our circumstance' (*Brutus* 24.112, 35.132). A similar disjunction is perceptible concerning *Oeconomicus*. Following upon a general recommendation of Xenophon's writings as 'extremely useful on many matters' and encouragement towards their study, Cato, speaking for Cicero, proceeds to cite a passage directly from the *Oeconomicus* to illustrate its commendation of hands-on husbandry (*On Old Age* 17.59). By contrast, after noting briefly the principles laid out for managing property in *Oeconomicus*, writing in his own voice in *On Duties*, Cicero suggests that on matters of investment it might be more profitable to consult moneylenders than any philosopher (2.87). Finally, Xenophon's/Prodicus' depiction of Hercules choosing whether to follow a life of Virtue or Vice is dismissed as fantasy. Normally, decisions regarding what path to pursue are ingrained following the custom of one's parents, or made by following the crowd, or set by chance or nature (17.117–18.121). Even men of exceptional quality and learning who also have the leisure to reflect are advised to choose according to the latter. In a work devoted to his son's erudition that recommends attention to Greek and Latin philosophy, including his own (1.1–2), this Roman thinker trumps the Greek philosopher's route towards virtue. Not all of Xenophon's lessons can or should be applied.

Emulation

Cicero's lively critical involvement with Xenophon's writings goes beyond any other Roman response and at the same time attests to the broad circulation of his works and ideas. This industry became more pronounced and, in the literary record, more prominent during the so-called Second Sophistic. From the mid-first to mid-third centuries AD, Xenophon was amongst the ancient authors whose wisdom highly educated men sought to resurrect and replicate (as described by Philostratus, *Lives of the Philosophers* 1.481). The emulation at the heart of these labours is encapsulated by Arrian of Nicomedia (AD 86–160), whose engagement with Xenophon was personal and sustained. The terms of this relationship are set out clearly in the opening section of Arrian's treatise *On Hunting*. Not only does the author declare his purpose to update Xenophon's work of the same title, but he justifies this based upon their shared name and citizenship and their joint interests in hunting, generalship and wisdom (1.4). Whether or not Xenophon was Arrian's actual name, befitting the Greek heritage of the Roman citizen Lucius Flavius Arrianus, or an adopted sobriquet, is a matter of debate. Either way, calling it to mind is a deliberate act of association, extended by the additional details on residency – Arrian settled in Athens in the late 130s after a distinguished senatorial and military career – and preoccupations. Furthermore, with the established goal of enhancing pre-circulating knowledge on the topic of hunting, Arrian explicitly follows the approach taken by Xenophon, when promises to build upon Simon's knowledge in his treatise *On Horsemanship* (1.5 ~ Xen. *Eq.* 1.1). Xenophon's implicit one-upmanship is co-opted by Arrian in *On Hunting* and oriented around the earlier author, whose understanding is both incorporated (cited, quoted) and critiqued (supplemented, over-written). It is now Arrian whose work will be judged 'useful'. Thus, Arrian's emulation is one of industry. However, in attempting a literary and intellectual feat analogous to Xenophon's original work, it is also an act of self-promotion that sets Arrian into retrospective competition with his namesake.

This competitive element, moreover, extends outwards to Arrian's contemporaries. The Second Sophistic was an agonistic environment. With participation depending upon an education that was the preserve of wealthy men of leisure, each written production became a performance by the author of his attainment and therefore also his status. So, when Arrian produced the eight-book *Discourses of Epictetus* as a memorial (*hupomnêmata*) to his teacher (Preface), he not only adapted the format of Xenophon's *Memorabilia* (in Greek *apomnêmoneumata*, from the same *mnêm-* stem) to fit the philosopher's discursive mode and instruction, but demonstrated his ability to do so. However, Arrian was not the only one playing with the form. Around the same time, the Gallic writer Favorinus (*c.* A D 85–155) also produced a *Memorabilia* (*Hupomnêmata*). Although it is now lost, a citation by Diogenes Laertius in his biography of Empedocles (*Lives of Eminent Philosophers* 8.53) suggests it contained anecdotes about those first-generation philosophers from the sixth to fourth centuries B C; it may also have included more personal reminiscences. With multiple individuals engaged in comparable ventures, and each one composing their own intellectual response to 'ancient' material, every display was inherently competitive: even if the game was played in the long term across a broad geographical terrain, following the circulation of texts between people and cities around the Roman Mediterranean over the centuries, and there was no declared winner or loser.

The stratification between educated men and those who lacked the training and therefore skill to compete was heightened by the preference for writing in an Attic style. Here again, by modelling himself and his writing on Xenophon, Arrian obtains a win. Although only one amongst several classical Athenians deemed worthy of imitation, Xenophon was singled out for the 'simplicity' and 'sweetness' and 'purity' of his prose (see Hermogenes, *On Types of Style* 2.12.4–10). To copy linguistic features of Xenophon's sentences such as vocabulary, syntax, morphology and dialect was to incorporate these qualities into one's own writing. Given that Attic Greek was effectively a dead language now that 'common' (*koinê*) Greek was the universal form of communication, this was a demanding task. It was not only Arrian's intellectual engagement with Xenophon's *oeuvre* (manifest also in his *Periplus*, the *Anabasis* of Alexander the Great, and *The Order of the Battle against the Alans*), but his style that made Arrian a 'new Xenophon'. Whatever the origins of the name, this is how he came to be known. For the ninth-century Byzantine scholar Photius who records this fact, it is 'in the plainness of his expression (that) he is a true imitator of Xenophon'. Befitting this, Arrian's own prose 'lacks neither rhetorical skill nor power' (*Library* 58 17b).

For the intellectual elite around the Roman empire, trained in Greek, Xenophon was thus a source of inspiration and imitation. Form and style were key. However, imitation also allowed for elaboration and invention. *Table Talk* by Plutarch of Chaeronea (*c.* AD 50–120) directly refers to the *Symposia* of Plato and Xenophon as models for both enjoying conversation over wine and recalling it (686d; the verb is this time *memnêsthai*). However, the ten-book presentation of topics discussed by Plutarch and his companions not only prioritizes one strand of the sympotic entertainments available at Callias' house (depicted by Xenophon), and gives his guests a dizzying array of topics by comparison to the discrete focus on love amongst Agathon's guest (in Plato's work). It is also framed as a series of letters. The two earlier *Symposia*, which already have spurred many philosophical efforts in the interim (see 612d), are trumped by the scale of Plutarch's reminiscences, garnered from many different gatherings of educated men. These include Plutarch's own contributions, replete with quotations from many earlier writers, including Xenophon.

The first conversation in book 2 is particularly illuminating. Here, Xenophon's *Cyropaedia* is in fact the stimulus, when Sossius Senecio (who is also the letter's addressee) uses Gobryas' admiration for the conviviality of the Persians to initiate consideration of the best topics at a drinking party. Plutarch, acting as respondent (and who is the actual author of the piece), immediately cites Xenophon as an authority (630a). Evidence from *Cyropaedia* and *Symposium* then follows. However, this is presented in order to construct an entirely independent line of argument. Hence, the gentle teasing of Sambaulus' ugly lover and Socrates' proposal that Critobulus join him in a beauty competition are proof that a joke might bring pleasure when its premises are clearly false (Plutarch, *Table Talk* 632a–b ~ Xen. *Cyr.* 2.2.28ff, *Symp.* 4.19–20). Combined with quotations from epic poetry, Athenian drama and philosophy, and historical exempla, this further illustrates a preference for conversations centred on success rather than on failure and for jokes that avoid giving offence. While Xenophon is woven into the fabric of this sympotic conversation, it is Plutarch's erudition and acumen that is proven.

Thus, while the works of Xenophon set the terms of their own emulation, they did not limit it. In the hands of Lucian of Samosata (born *c.* AD 120), those works could even be subverted. *The Dream, or Lucian's Career* is a parody of the Choice of Heracles (Xen. *Mem.* 2.1.21–34). Described on the premise it will be 'useful' to listeners – allegedly the reason that Xenophon reported the dream of a thunderbolt striking his father's house (Lucian, *The Dream* 17 ~ Xen. *An.* 3.1.11–14) –, the night-time visitation from Education and Sculpture crystallizes the decision young Lucian must make between continuing in the classroom or embarking upon a manual career. From their first appearance, this is a comic version. Instead of launching into grand speeches, the two women attempt to physically wrestle Lucian to their side (6). When they turn to persuasion, each promises praise and fame (7). Education, speaking at greater length and with eloquence, refutes Sculpture by sketching two possible lives. In the first, the bodily toil of a worker will leave Lucian unremarkable and diminished; lacking means and mental resource for himself, he will need to toady to better educated men. In the second, Lucian will possess the virtues of 'moderation, justice, piety, fairness, wit, and endurance, love of beauty and an impetus towards august affairs'. Moreover, as Education's protégé, he will be envied and esteemed and called upon for help in times of trouble (10–12). Education's promises do not parallel those of Virtue in *Memorabilia* specifically, but they do resonate closely with the virtues embodied by Socrates and the life recommended to his young associates in that work (see Chapter 4).

However, this elevated vision is undercut by an apathetic audience: 'long-winded pettifogging', 'old news' and 'stale' are its judgement (17). Other elements of *The Dream* are equally destabilizing. The speaker cannot remember much of Sculpture's argument (8). Plus, far from regarding the dream as divinely inspired (as the *Anabasis* comparison might suggest), the entire episode is rationalized as the result of a beating received by Lucian earlier in the day from his uncle, a sculptor to whom he is apprenticed (16). The closing message might seem inspiring: that by taking the narrator as a model (*paradeigma*, the same word used by Xenophon for Socrates, Cyrus and Agesilaus), a poor man might embrace education. However, even this is undercut in the closing evaluation: 'for if nothing else, I am less disreputable than a sculptor' (18). Lucian's pseudo-autobiography not only undermines itself, but cuts at the pretensions at the heart of the Choice narrative, which is deployed so seriously by Xenophon's Socrates (reportedly the son of a stone worker: Diogenes Laertius 2.18). Xenophon thus serves Lucian in his wider project to challenge the self-regarding enterprise of the Second Sophistic through demonstrations of mastery that include warped imitation.

Transmission

The extended flurry of industry around Xenophon's written works amongst educated men living under the Roman Empire was symptomatic of a distinctive literary and intellectual culture. Despite the various social, religious and political changes that unsettled and eventually led to the disintegration of the Roman Empire, Xenophon continued to be useful. Perhaps surprisingly, in *Preparation for the Gospel* Eusebius (*c.* AD 260–339), described him as 'the most distinguished of Socrates' companions', before quoting from *Memorabilia*. This, however, was a loaded move. At this point in his refutation of pagan theology, the bishop of Caesarea is intent not just upon dismissing earlier theories about the formation of the cosmos and location of the soul, but the validity and utility of such investigations. To do this, Eusebius calls upon Xenophon's portrait of Socrates, 'the wisest of the Greeks' who also rejected investigations into the natural world (*Preparation for the Gospel* 15.61–2 ~ Xen. *Mem.* 1.1.11). The great reputation of Socrates and Xenophon validates Eusebius' argument against their fellow pagan philosophers. Furthermore, aside from its Christian frame, Eusebius' preference for moral philosophy looks strikingly close to the model promoted by Xenophon: dedicated to useful endeavours, 'we hold only to piety concerning God who made everything and, through a moderate (*sôphronos*) life, seek by the virtue (*aretê*) beloved of God in other daily affairs to pursue a life that is pleasing to the God of all' (see Chapter 4). To some degree, Eusebius is playing the same old game. Along with the myriad Greek authors cited by Eusebius, Xenophon's incorporation into his theological discourse conveys learning and authority. However, the singular divinity signals a shift. By demonstrating the rectitude of Christian theology, Xenophon and Socrates are sublimated to Eusebius' world view.

The background context here is the competition between proponents of the new state religion and adherents to what was now described as paganism. For Eunapius of Sardis (born *c.* AD 345), on the other side of the debate, Xenophon was a definitive point of reference when compiling his resistance piece. Intended to counter Christianity's hagiographic traditions, *Lives of the Sophists* opened with praise of Xenophon as exceptional for 'adorning philosophy with words and deeds'. Although Eunapius skews his attention towards serious accomplishments rather than moments of play, Xenophon's ambition to record the incidental activities of worthy men is an authorizing device that simultaneously connects Eunapius to the longer tradition of writing philosopher's lives (*Lives of the Sophists* 453 ~ Xen. *Symp.* 1.1). However, the remains of a papyrus scroll from Egypt point to a sadder and more ubiquitous fate (*P.Mich.* 4922; see Figure 5.1). The two surviving fragments contain portions of Xenophon's

Figure 5.1 Papyrus fragments featuring Xenophon's *Cyropaedia*, overwritten by a Christian text (*P.Mich.* inv. 4922). Photograph from the Advanced Papyrological Information System, University of Michigan. © University of Michigan Library. https://quod.lib.umich.edu/a/apis/x-2344/*.

Cyropaedia, book 2. By handwriting, these can be dated to the first or second century A D. At some point in the fourth or fifth century, the scroll was dismantled. This strip was then used for jotting down thoughts on the biblical book of Exodus in every available space and even on top of the original text, as if it were scrap paper. The physical dismemberment and overwriting of Xenophon's work is symbolic of the wider process of elision which removed the author, and Greek literature more broadly, from general circulation.

Xenophon, of course, did not entirely disappear. Following the collapse of Roman power in western Europe and north Africa, knowledge of ancient Greek continued in the East, and especially Byzantium (Constantinople), where the Roman empire held on, albeit under near-constant assault and mainly in retreat. Traces of Xenophon are evident in two large-scale compilations: the *Library* written by Photius during the mid-ninth century and the lexicon known as the *Suda*, produced in the tenth. Both carry forward the same idea of Xenophon, associating him with Socrates and other famous contemporaries, observing his Attic style, and showing awareness, to varying degrees, of his connection with the younger Cyrus (Photius, *Library* cod. 243 372b, 260 486b, 158 101b; *Suda sv* Xenophon ξ 47, 48). However, while Photius does appear aware of Xenophon as the author of *Anabasis*, it takes the later *Suda* to identify him explicitly as a writer of philosophical lives (*apomnêmoneumata*) and the author of particular texts: *Cyropaedia, Anabasis, Hellenica* and *Symposium* and 'many others'. The manuscript tradition also supports the circulation of Xenophon's works at this time. For example, in the mid-tenth century a codex was produced that by the fourteenth century, after two separate restorations and supplementations, would contain *Cyropaedia, Anabasis, Apology, Agesilaus, Hiero, Constitution of the Lacedaemonians*, the spuriously attributed *Constitution of the Athenians*, and an incomplete version of *On Hunting* (Vaticanus gr. 1335 (A)). Notably, it lacks the three other Socratic works and the treatises on revenues, cavalry command and horses, which several fourteenth-century manuscripts bring together in different combinations, sometimes alongside selected works by different authors (e.g. Plutarch and Arrian: Marcianus gr. 511 (M)). Nonetheless, this 246-page book constitutes the oldest surviving collection of Xenophon's works. As such, it speaks to longer-term labours in gathering and copying and reading ancient texts, within a flourishing literary and scholastic culture, centred upon the imperial court at Byzantium. However, the manuscript's eventual incorporation into the library of the renowned Italian humanist and collector of classical antiquities, Fulvio Orsini and, on his death in 1600, into the Vatican collection, also highlights Xenophon's transition into the intellectual life of members of the educated male elite in western Europe. The context is, of course, the Renaissance.

Rebirth

Xenophon's route from Byzantium to Italy at the turn of the fifteenth century was the standard one for Greek authors, brought about by the clamour for classical texts that followed a lively period of re-engagement with Latin literature and learning ('Humanism') and sustained by the arrival of Byzantine scholars. Whilst learning ancient Greek would remain a niche scholarly activity, widening accessibility was facilitated by the first translations into Latin, a universal language in education and diplomacy, and then into the vernacular. Xenophon's *Cyropaedia*, for example, was translated thirteen times into Latin. The first complete version – at least complete in scope; it was still compressed and written in paraphrase – was produced by the Florentine humanist Poggio Bracciolini in 1447. This quickly became the basis for translations in Italian (by Poggio's son Jacopo, 1476) and French (by Vasco da Lucena, 1470). In the next century, fresh translations of varying lengths and exactitude followed in German (Hieronymus Boner, 1540), French (Jacques de Vintimille, 1547), English (William Barker, 1552), and Spanish (Diego Gracían, 1552). By this time, *Cyropaedia* was the standard text for learning Greek, and dissemination was aided by the new technology of the printing press. However, its popularity also lay in the assumed applicability of the Persian king Cyrus' education to the modern political world.

The aspiration that the new translations would be of value in moulding rulers is expressed in their frequent dedication to noble patrons. For example, the French translation by da Lucena, a diplomat in service to Isabella of Portugal, was gifted in the first instance to her son, the duke of Burgundy, Charles the Bold. A copy was also presented around the same time to a visiting (and temporarily dethroned) Edward IV of England, whose sister was the duke's third wife. A prefatory statement emphasizes the relevance: 'here begins the first book of the history of the Persian king Cyrus, composed by the philosopher Xenophon and entitled "on very good monarchy"' (London, British Museum, Royal 16 G IX, fol. 10). Notably, the Burgundian ruler was reading this alongside translations of Xenophon's *Hiero* (produced on commission by Charles Soillot in 1460 from the Latin version by Leonardo Bruni, 1403), Julius Caesar's *Gallic Wars* (translated by Jehan du Chesne, 1472), and Quintus Curtius' *Alexander the Great* (also by da Lucena, *c.* 1468–75). The exemplarity of Cyrus as monarch, along with the Macedonian and Roman generals, appealed to Europe's ruling aristocracy who were embattled, like their ancient predecessors, in territorial wars of expansion. Indeed, the application of Cyrus' organizational principles has even been argued for the Burgundian army.

However, as da Lucena informs his addressee, and alluding to Cicero, it was to demonstrate the qualities of a just monarch that Xenophon wrote about Cyrus. After all, it was the example of a virtuous king that led Alexander, Scipio and others to read about him.

As a model, *Cyropaedia* thus works in two ways. Where Cyrus argued that he and his companions must be models in virtue to one another and the next generation (~Xen. *Cyr.* 7.5.85–6), the duke can use that model to reflect on appropriate ways to govern. Plus, by reading *Cyropaedia*, he can mimic those great generals too. However, the hope of the author that his own work 'is not of a little use' (Preface, fol. 8/9) reveals that there is more at play than flattering royal vanity. The translator thus makes his own bid to be a wise advisor at court, offering up the words of Xenophon for contemplation and action. It is a dynamic enshrined in colourful illustration above the written dedication on the richly decorated luxury manuscript: the enthroned ruler receiving the book from the translator, who, on bended knee, offers up the results of his labour (fol. 7). The resemblance between Charles the Bold surrounded by courtiers in this scene and one later in which Cyrus observes Chrysantas addressing troops dressed in plate armour emphasizes the point (fol. 169; see Figure 5.2): follow this guidance and you can be Cyrus.

A rather more critical engagement with Cyrus and the wider 'mirror for princes' genre can be found in *The Prince*, written by Niccolò Machiavelli. Completed by the Italian political philosopher in 1513 and published posthumously in 1532, *The Prince* takes as its impetus an ambition to share 'knowledge of the actions of great men' (p. 18, tr. W. K. Marriot), with whom the author has become familiar through life and study, with its dedicant, Lorenzo the Magnificent, head of Florence's powerful De' Medici family. Cyrus is brought into the debate when attention turns to war, 'the sole art that belongs to him who rules' (p. 57). First, the key tenets of a Persian education and Cyrus' reforms of the Persian army (Xen. *Cyr.* 1.2.9–11, 2.1.11–31) are implicit in the promotion of hunting as essential training for the physical toils of war for a young prince and in the need to organize and drill the troops. Second, Cyrus is one of the 'illustrious men' whose defeats and victories recorded in historical accounts must be

Figure 5.2 Folio from an illustrated manuscript of the translation of Xenophon's *Cyropaedia* by Vasco da Lucena (*c.* 1470–83). British Library Royal 16 G IX fol. 169. © The British Library.

studied in order to work out strategies to imitate or avoid. With echoes of Cicero and da Lucena (likely via the Latin translation by Poggio), the prime exemplar is the Roman general Scipio. However, he is recommended not only in his own right, but as a reader and imitator of Xenophon's Cyrus, through whom 'chastity, affability, humanity and liberality' were reached (p. 58). Elements of Xenophon's representation of Cyrus are extracted and are integrated into Machiavelli's analysis.

Xenophon's wider thinking on virtuous leadership is also implicit in recommendations on how a prince should behave. However, by introducing room for negotiation, Machiavelli turns several cherished principles on their heads. For example, in 'Concerning things for which men, and especially princes, are praised or blamed' (§15), vice is endorsed, if it helps a prince secure his position (p. 59). This goes well beyond the advice from Cambyses that Cyrus might learn deceit, now he has mastered justice, in order to pursue advantage: as Cyrus puts it, 'to do good and bad to men' (Xen. *Cyr.* 1.6.27–40, quoting 1.1.30). By Machiavelli's rationale, human nature prohibits any one person from possessing every virtue, so an informed balance between right and wrong is a more practical approach to maintaining power. Alternatively, 'Concerning liberality and meanings' (§16), the generosity that Cyrus, Caesar and Alexander were known to have displayed by distributing booty to the troops must be balanced against the danger of acquiring a reputation for rapacity, which may incur blame (p. 62). Finally, 'Concerning clemency, and whether it is better to be loved than feared' (§17), the latter is sometimes better: a notion Cambyses implicitly rejects when he dismisses unwilling obedience instilled by punishment in preference for willing obedience generated by the granting of favours (~ Xen. *Cyr.* 1.6.20–1). The justification is that killing one person might avert danger to the community. Where seizing property and killing without just cause are to be avoided, it is because these actions will engender fear *and* hatred: the position the tyrant of Syracuse needs advice to get himself out of in Xenophon's *Hiero*. Crucially, cruelty will not win loyalty amongst the army, but neither will an easy attitude: points underpinning Xenophon's portraits of Clearchus and Proxenus (Xen. *Anabasis* 2.6.9–12, 2.6.19–20).

In sum, Machiavelli appears to be thinking through models of leadership encountered in Xenophon and considering their viability in practice. On the one hand, the continual in-fighting between Italian city-states meant that Machiavelli's world was not so entirely distant from Xenophon's fractious fourth-century Greece. But for Machiavelli virtue is not always possible or desirable. Hence, it is more important to appear virtuous: the deceit permitted to rulers extending also to an appearance of honesty (§18). This is, of course, inimical to Xenophon's entire project, where imitation of the virtuous is a route to virtue. In *The Prince,* while Xenophon's Cyrus merits imitation in matters of war, a cunning evaluation of the benefits of virtue is better suited to reality.

To this pessimism, *The Travels of Cyrus,* written by the Scot Andrew Ramsay and published for the first time in 1727, is a tonic. It too presented the future Persian king as a model of good rulership, in this case to Ramsay's former pupil, Prince Charles Edward Stuart (known also as Bonnie Prince Charlie, the Young Pretender). However, the story of Cyrus' education was rewritten entirely. Although it begins with Cyrus' sojourn at the court of Astyages in Media (~ Xen. *Cyr.* 1.3.1–1.4.28), *Travels* diverges at this point by making Cyrus fall in love. Following in the tradition of mediaeval romances, a 'noble Passion' for a virtuous princess becomes the root of Cyrus' own virtue (pp. 28–9). United once obstacles are overcome, particularly Cassandana's engagement to Cyrus' evil cousin Cyaxares, the married couple together travel to join the Magi. Here, after hearing about his romantic travails, they receive instruction in natural philosophy from Zoroaster, which connects Virtue in life with Immortality of the soul (book 2). And this is how the *Travels* continues, with Cyrus mimicking the travelling sages of antiquity by seeking knowledge in foreign lands: in Egypt, Greece, Crete and Babylon. Conversations with local men, whose knowledge and experience shed light on aspects of government, political organization and religious philosophy, form the basis of Cyrus' education.

Within this creative riff on the *Cyropaedia*, however, there is still room for Xenophon. For example, as Amenophis relates the fluctuations in his own fortunes to Cyrus, he also describes the predicament of two Egyptian kings. The first, Apries, distrusted the wrong man. Thus, after imprisoning the well-meaning Amenophis, he found himself deposed by the duplicitous Amasis, who had engineered support from the masses by encouraging Apries to rule absolutely, thus earning their hatred. Amasis in turn ruled 'with Mildness and Moderation'. However, knowledge of his own deceit meant he could not enjoy happiness. The problems experienced by the Egyptian kings are exactly those encountered by tyrants in Xenophon's *Hiero* (see Chapter 3). Where the Syracusan tyrant bemoans a lack of friends, Amenophis makes clear that friendship is impossible for kings; this is the primary lesson Cyrus takes away from his encounter (pp. 124, 145 ~ Xen. *Hiero* 3.1–9). Furthermore, 'the Happiness of the People . . . makes the Happiness of the Prince', Amenophis remarks, echoing Simonides' advice on devoting oneself to the common good (p. 144 ~ Xen. *Hiero* 11.15). Appropriately, then, Cyrus leaves behind his new friend and commits to his ordained fate in order 'that I may contribute to the Happiness of my country' (p. 154). Through Amenophis' autobiographical tale, Ramsay's Cyrus learns the lesson that Xenophon's Simonides offers Hiero. So too might Charles Edward Stuart. Pointed warnings about populist appeals to the will of the people, the fickleness of the masses and the need for appeasement to avoid revolution are also packaged into this episode, as appropriate to the period and the intended beneficiary. Although living in Rome, the Stuart family still plotted to reclaim the British throne from which they had been deposed in 1688 as absolutist (Catholic) monarchs, antagonistic to parliamentary rule. If the Young Pretender is to claim his throne, he will need to navigate the line between autocracy and populism. Xenophon's thinking is threaded into Ramsay's wider advice to the exiled prince and would-be future king.

Revival

By conceit, the 'mirror for princes' genre offered individuals a glimpse of the ruler they could be, if they just followed the model provided. Xenophon's Cyrus remained a popular reflection. However, his refraction (side-lined by Machiavelli, reinvented by Ramsay) mirrored changing times and perspectives. Since the twentieth century, Xenophon has undergone similar transformations. Following upon the adoption of *Anabasis* as a school text in the nineteenth century, the reception of Xenophon is now dominated by fictionalizations of the *Anabasis*. As the hero of his own account, Xenophon has become a cipher for the morality of war. Take, for example, Geoffrey Household's 1955 retelling of the *Anabasis* for young readers. As indicated by the two titles under which it was published – *Xenophon's Adventure* and *The Exploits of Xenophon* – Household made Xenophon the protagonist in an action-filled tale of struggle against adversity. Furthermore, with the story now told in the first person, the advance and retreat of the Greek army are matters of personal experience. Every word uttered by Xenophon reveals his thinking; every action defines his character. Thus, the challenge to Xenophon, remaining on horseback as his troops run towards the summit, is met by a personal response: 'I jumped off my horse, shoved Soterides out of the line and took his shield. It nearly finished me' (p. 63 ~ Xen. *An.* 3.4.44–9). Or, winding through the Kurdish mountains, 'I had a narrow escape. The enemy were hot on our tail; they rolled down rocks again, uttering terrifying yells' (p. 72 ~ Xen. *An.* 4.2.20–1). Such focalization heightens the sense of danger and amplifies the character Xenophon's courage and endurance. The march into and out of Persia thus becomes a series of military encounters during which Xenophon acts bravely. The all-action hero displays traditional values for 'improving' stories aimed at boys during the heyday of the British Empire. At the same time, describing how the charge of the Greeks 'was too much for the *natives*'

(p. 33) at Cunaxa, 'the *natives* broke and fled' when Xenophon and his men took the summit (p. 63), and dinner in Thrace 'was good in a *primitive* way' (p. 146) (my emphases), he surveys the locals with an imperialist eye. For all that he follows the trajectory set by *Anabasis*, in the *Adventure/Exploits* Xenophon is essentially a hero of empire, who returns home safely to Athens from a jolly old adventure in foreign lands.

This ideological reworking of Xenophon is particularly striking because it appeared at the very time the British Empire was crumbling, and only a decade after the end of World War II, during which Britons had experienced at first hand the deprivations, degradations and moral complications of war. Looking back with nostalgia to an age of conquest and easy-to-define heroism, *Xenophon's Adventure* reflects an era that had already passed (and arguably, as a product of the imperialist imagination, never really existed). Although it might not yet have been fully apparent, Household's Xenophon was a defunct model.

Conversely, the comic book *400 BC: The Story of the Ten Thousand* (2010), written by the American Lewis Helfand, very much belongs in the twenty-first century. In look, Xenophon conforms to the muscle-bound hunk familiar to Hollywood film. On his first appearance, standing with a spear in one hand and helmet in the other, he draws the viewer's gaze and dominates the page. Yet, captions in the corners raise questions about his identity. Rumours make him an ordinary soldier with high-ranking friends, 'but why do the generals seem to trust his counsel?' (p. 10). Xenophon must win over the soldiers who are forced, by circumstance, to accept him as leader. This he attempts by driving the men on (p. 35), taking hard decisions (p. 37), rousing them to flight (pp. 39–41), lashing out at those who abandon their comrades (p. 42), securing provisions (p. 52), recovering stolen money from Seuthes (p. 60), leading the soldiers into fight after fight (p. 53, pp. 64–5), and bringing them safely to Thibron (p. 64). During the march, in a series of episodes that serve a similar purpose in *Anabasis* (see Chapter 1), Xenophon shows himself to be a valiant and effective leader of men.

However, in this retelling, the main character is the man who is ultimately won over after expressing those initial concerns: Eustachius. As told in flash-back, it is Eustachius (not Xenophon ~ *An.* 3.1.4) who is persuaded by his friend Aeneas to join the campaign and seek his fortune. As a poor farmer who must support the family of a brother killed in war, Eustachius has no choice (pp. 21–5). Over the course of the journey, Eustachius gives voice to the physical and emotional suffering of the soldiers: the weary limbs, the thirst and hunger, and the loss of his friend (p. 35, p. 46). Sitting isolated when the soldiers celebrate reaching the sea, he thinks only of home (p. 50). For the man caught up in the lashing rain and falling snow, panel after panel (pp. 38–47), this is no adventure. Rather, with Eustachius recording their reduction from 100,000 soldiers to 10,000 to six thousand in captions, while in illustration the remaining troops fight onwards, this is attrition. Thus, Xenophon is decentred from his own story. In his place, an ordinary soldier provides the emotional core. This new version is still about bravery and endurance, but also suffering. It is also about the ethics of war. With scenes of combat and talk of 'brothers' (in arms), the comic book sustains a notion of heroism familiar to popular culture depictions of soldiers at war. Indeed, in the very final scene, Eustachius comforts Aeneas' son with the usual platitudes about how his father 'lives on in the memories of the Greek army'. However, the final caption articulates the soldier's dilemma. 'If you live by the sword, you will die by the sword. Is that how I will meet my end, if I go to war again?', ponders Eustachius (p. 68). Reflecting a strengthened rhetoric of militarism and a wider discomfort with (unjustified: see the deceit of Cyrus on p. 9) military adventure in the United States, post-9/11, war is fetishized and critiqued. Crucially, Xenophon the general is irrelevant here. In this democratized retelling, it is one of the *Anabasis*' voiceless many who provides a means to think through the complexities of war.

Conclusion

The reception of Xenophon is thus characterized by continuity and diversity. Just as his writings form the basis for a developing biography – as discussed in the Introduction; in fact, this is part of the reception story – they provide the stimulus and content for new inquiries and expositions. Here, the idea of Xenophon is also important, as a source of authority and self-affirmation. From Rome through to the present, individual responses to Xenophon and his work are driven by the contemporary intellectual, cultural, and socio-political environment as well as their author's philosophical and political aspirations. Different works have different appeal and usage. Xenophon's own modelling of Cyrus in *Cyropaedia* has facilitated further remodelling within contexts where leadership poses challenges: when the Romans must administer the conquered territories they are consolidating into an empire, or when early modern European aristocrats seek to carve out their own kingdoms one against the other. The Socratic dialogues offer propositions that can be harvested and redeployed, in a straightforward or critical fashion, while the form itself offers stimulus to new portraits of philosophers in action and fresh philosophical investigations. Opportunities are limited only by the creativity and imagination of the writer and their own horizons. So, in Late Antiquity, Christians and pagans could each find self-justification for their understandings and endeavours in the portraits of Socrates. And in modern retellings, the *Anabasis* can celebrate and undercut war. Within the constraints that make his contributions distinctive, Xenophon affords flexibility in engagement, enabling new answers to his underlying questions about politics and morality.

Conclusion

The Stranger's Voice

Xenophon was a prolific writer and provocative thinker. His primary talent lay in dramatizing encounters between historical individuals characterized by verbal exchange. These Xenophon wove into longer narratives about people and events or moulded into detailed conversations to provide insights on human affairs. His underpinning interests in politics and morality were also developed through problem-oriented discussions that recommend actions for cities regarding their organization and for citizens regarding conduct. Across this literary terrain, Xenophon moves in and out of view. Sometimes, an opening gambit frames the coming work within a wider field of investigation undertaken to a stated purpose; sometimes the author intervenes with an evaluation or reflection that affords interpretation; and sometimes he explicitly steers the content. As the mode of inquiry shifts between dramatization and didacticism, Xenophon permits an open engagement with the issues raised, whilst encouraging a particular take: on the best way to organize a community, on the qualities required for leadership, on the values associated with virtue (for example).

Xenophon's unfolding scenarios also have a two-way effect of drawing readers into other times and places, whilst establishing them as external spectators. The second effect is exacerbated by the distance of those imagined worlds from the present-day experience of the reader. The dilemmas, decisions and debates to which Xenophon brings his readers up-close frequently take place outwith their ken:

during the so-called 'golden age' of Socrates or within the deep past of the Persian empire or at Sparta. Thus, the man whose name means 'foreign voice' invites his reader to join him on the edges of propriety. To celebrate Persia, to laud Sparta and its king, to rehabilitate the controversial sophist: all are inimical to the dominant self-positioning of Xenophon's hometown, where Persia is always an effete other, Sparta is the eternal enemy, and Socrates was executed because of his malign influence. Certainly, Athens has always had its Medizers and its pro-Spartan sympathizers, and Xenophon is not alone in his Socratic project. Thus, Xenophon's perspective is not entirely alien to men of his class. Nor is he unequivocal in praise of the 'other'. Moreover, the problems that he addresses and his modes of writing develop within a wider tradition of Greek thinking. Having spent years in the territory and company of Persians and Spartans (remembering that the Spartans are Greeks, albeit, by his account, exceptional ones), Xenophon makes interventions into ongoing conversations over matters of political and philosophical concern from the outside and within.

Reading Xenophon in the twenty-first century, the world conjured by his various writings stand at an even greater remove. Yet, because he interrogates aspects of human existence, his works still resonate. Nonetheless, shared general concerns cannot override the strangeness to us of Xenophon's specific political, social and moral worldview. Cyrus' benevolent autocracy; Sparta's brutal surveillance society; the foundation of Athens' economic success upon slavery; the justified confinement of women within a domestic role. Not to mention the uncontemplated fates of women packaged up and portioned out as rewards to the younger Cyrus' followers; and the violence and death that the Ten Thousand meted out on people who resisted their invasion. Such features sit uneasily with the principles of freedom and equality to which modern western democracies commit themselves, even if these are only partially established at home and frequently forgotten when dealing with other nations. To read Xenophon is to be discomfited.

Despite this, in some respects Xenophon seems surprisingly modern. By contrast to Aristotle's equation of women and children and slaves in mental competence (*Politics* 1260a), Xenophon recognizes the capacity for moral agency relating to household management amongst slaves and women as well as their masters and husbands. Likewise, in Cyrus' meritocracy at least, lowborn men can climb the ranks, when afforded the opportunity. However, while the egalitarian sentiments might seem familiar, again the terms of their expression mark them apart. Xenophon's world is not our own, nor do his responses to its problems gel with twenty-first sensibilities. Even still, by opening up questions of continuing relevance, Xenophon affords perspectives to clarify our own thinking. For example, in an age of populism and when the very qualities that make a good leader are contested, might a commitment to benefiting one's fellow citizens offer an appropriate basis for action? Or, at a time of climate change and ecological emergency, how can individuals be persuaded to contribute to top-down initiatives aimed at the common good? Or, when technology permits governments unprecedented capabilities to survey their citizens, what are the implications for democracies? Well beyond his own imagining, Xenophon's writing may still be useful today.

Further Reading

Translations

Ambler, W., 2001, *Xenophon: The Education of Cyrus*, Ithaca: Cornell University Press.

Ambler, W., 2008, *Xenophon: The Anabasis of Cyrus*, Ithaca: Cornell University Press.

Bartlett, R., 1996, *Xenophon: The Shorter Socratic Writings*, Ithaca: Cornell University Press.

Bonnette, A. L., 1994, *Xenophon: Memorabilia*, Ithaca: Cornell University Press.

Bowen, A. J., 1999, *Xenophon: Symposium*, Warminster: Aris and Phillips.

Krentz, P., 1989, *Xenophon: Hellenica I-II.3.10*, Warminster: Aris and Phillips.

Krentz, P., 1995, *Xenophon: Hellenica II.3.11–IV.2.8*, Warminster: Aris and Phillips.

Macleod, M. D., 2008, *Xenophon: Apology and Memorabilia I*, Warminster: Aris and Phillips.

McBrayer, G. (ed.), 2018, *Xenophon: The Shorter Writings*, Ithaca: Cornell University Press.

Phillips, A. A. and M. M. Wilcock, 1999, *Xenophon and Arrian on Hunting*, Warminster: Aris & Phillips.

Tredennick, H. and R. Waterfield, 1990, *Xenophon: Conversations of Socrates*, London: Penguin.

Warner, R., 1949, *Xenophon: The Persian Expedition*, Harmondsworth: Penguin.

Warner, R., 1966, *Xenophon: A History of My Times (Hellenica)*, Harmondsworth: Penguin.

Waterfield, R., 1997, *Xenophon: Hiero the Tyrant and Other Treatises*, London: Penguin.

Waterfield, R., 2005, *The Expedition of Cyrus*, Oxford: Oxford University Press.

On Xenophon

Anderson, J. K., 1974, *Xenophon*, London: Duckworth.

Dillery, J., 1995, *Xenophon and the History of his Times*, New York: Routledge.

Flower, M. (ed.), 2016, *The Cambridge Companion to Xenophon*, Cambridge: Cambridge University Press.

Gray, V. J. (ed.), 2010, *Xenophon*, Oxford: Oxford University Press.

Gray, V. J., 2011, *Xenophon's Mirror of Princes: Reading the Reflections*, Oxford: Oxford University Press.

Higgins, W. E., 1977, *Xenophon the Athenian: The Problem of the Individual and the Society of the Polis*, Albany: State University of New York Press.

On individual works

Morrison, D. R., 1988, *Bibliography of Editions, Translations, and Commentary on Xenophon's Socratic Writings, 1600–present*, Pittsburgh: Mathesis Publications.

Anabasis

Buzzetti, E., 2014, *Xenophon the Socratic Prince: The Argument of the Anabasis of Cyrus*, New York: Palgrave Macmillan.

Flower, M., 2012, *Xenophon's Anabasis, or, the Expedition of Cyrus*, Oxford: Oxford University Press.

Lane Fox, R. (ed.), 2004, *The Long March: Xenophon and the Ten Thousand*, New Haven: Yale University Press.

Nussbaum, G. B., 1967, *The Ten Thousand: A Study in Social Organization and Action in Xenophon's Anabasis*, Leiden: Brill.

Rood, T., 2004, *The Sea! The Sea! The Shout of the Ten Thousand in the Modern Imagination*, London: Duckworth Overlook.

Rood, T., 2010, *American Anabasis: Xenophon and the Idea of America from the Mexican War to Iraq*, London: Duckworth Overlook.

Waterfield, R., 2006, *Xenophon's Retreat: Greece, Persia and the End of the Golden Age*, London: Faber and Faber.

Constitution of the Lacedaemonians

Lipka, M., 2002, *Xenophon's Spartan Constitution: Introduction, Text, Commentary*, Berlin: De Gruyter.

Proietti, G., 1987, *Xenophon's Sparta: An Introduction*, Leiden: Brill.

Cyropaedia

Bodil, D., 1989, *The Cyropaedia: Xenophon's Aims and Methods*, Aarhus: Aarhus University Press.

Gera, D. L., 1993, *Xenophon's Cyropaedia: Style, Genre and Literary Technique*, Oxford: Clarendon Press.

Nadon, C., 2001, *Xenophon's Prince: Republic and Empire in Cyropaedia*, Berkeley: University of California Press.

Sandridge, N. B., 2012, *Loving Humanity, Learning, and Being Honored: The Foundations of Leadership in Xenophon's Education of Cyrus*, Washington DC: Centre for Hellenic Studies.

Tatum, J., 1989, *Xenophon's Imperial Fiction: On the Education of Cyrus*, Princeton: Princeton University Press.

Hellenica

Gray, V. J., 1989, *The Character of Xenophon's Hellenica*, London: Duckworth.

Kapellos, A., 2019, *Xenophon's Peloponnesian War*, Berlin: De Gruyter.

Marincola, J., 2009, *The Landmark Xenophon's Hellenika: A New Translation*, New York: Pantheon Books.

Tuplin, C. 1993. *The Failings of Empire: A Reading of Xenophon, Hellenica 2.3.11–7.5.27*, Stuttgart: F. Steiner Verlag.

Hiero

Strauss, L., 1948, *On Tyranny: An Interpretation of Xenophon's Hiero*, New York: Political Science Classics.

Memorabilia

Gray, V. J., 1998, *The Framing of Socrates: The Literary Interpretation of Xenophon's Memorabilia*, Stuttgart: F. Steiner Verlag.

Pangle, T. L., 2018, *The Socratic Way of Life: Xenophon's Memorabilia*, Chicago: University of Chicago Press.

Oeconomicus

Kronenberg, L., 2009, *Allegories of Farming from Greece and Rome: Philosophical Satire in Xenophon, Varro and Virgil*, Cambridge: Cambridge University Press.

Pomeroy, S. B., 1994, *Xenophon, Oeconomicus: A Social and Historical Commentary*, Oxford: Clarendon.

Strauss, L., 1970, *Xenophon's Socratic Discourse: An Interpretation of the Oeconomicus*, Ithaca: Cornell University Press.

On Horsemanship

Anderson, J. K., 1961, *Ancient Greek Horsemanship*, Berkeley: University of California Press.

Thematic studies

Persia

Hirsch, S., 1985, *The Friendship of the Barbarians: Xenophon and the Persian Empire*, Hanover: University Press of New England.

Philosophy

Danzig, G., 2010, *Apologizing for Socrates: How Plato and Xenophon created our Socrates*, Lanham: Lexington Books.

Danzig, G., D. Johnson and D. Morrison (eds), 2018, *Plato and Xenophon: Comparative Studies*, Leiden: Brill.

Houliang, L., 2015, *Xenophon's Theory of Moral Education*, Newcastle upon Tyne: Cambridge Scholars Press.

Stavru, A. and C. Moore (eds), 2018, *Socrates and the Socratic Dialogue*, Leiden: Brill.

Strauss, L., 1972, *Xenophon's Socrates*, Ithaca: Cornell University Press.

Politics

Azoulay, V., 2018, *Xenophon and the Graces of Power: A Greek Guide to Political Manipulation*, Swansea: Classical Press of Wales.

Buxton, R. F. (ed.), 2016, *Aspects of Leadership in Xenophon*, Newcastle upon Tyne: University of Newcastle.

Gish, D. and W. Ambler (eds), 2009, *The Political Thought of Xenophon*, Exeter: Imprint Academic.

Tamiolaki, M. (ed.), 2018, *Xenophon and Isocrates: Political Affinities and Literary Interactions*, Berlin: De Gruyter.

Various

Burliga, B. (ed.), 2011, *Xenophon: Greece, Persia, and Beyond*, Gdansk: Foundation of the Development of Gdansk University.

Hobden, F. and C. Tuplin (eds), 2012, *Xenophon: Ethical Principles and Historical Enquiry*, Leiden: Brill.

Kapellos, A. (ed.), 2019, *Xenophon on Violence*, Berlin De Gruyter.

Tuplin, C. (ed.), 2004, *Xenophon and his World: Papers from a Conference held in Liverpool in July 1999*, Stuttgart: F. Steiner Verlag.

Index